Build and

Build and Upgrade Your Own PC

Ian Sinclair

Newnes

OXFORD AUCKLAND BOSTON JOHANNESBURG MELBOURNE NEW DELHI

Newnes
An imprint of Butterworth-Heinemann
Linacre House, Jordan Hill, Oxford OX2 8DP
225 Wildwood Avenue, Woburn, MA 01801-2041
A division of Reed Educational and Professional Publishing Ltd

 A member of the Reed Elsevier plc group

First published 1999

British Library Cataloguing in Publication Data
A catalogue record for this book is available from the British Library

ISBN 07506 4267 X

Library of Congress Cataloguing in Publication Data
A catalogue record for this book is available from the Library of Congress

Typeset by David Gregson Associates, Beccles, Suffolk
Printed in Great Britain by Biddles, Guildford, Surrey

FOR EVERY TITLE THAT WE PUBLISH, BUTTERWORTH-HEINEMANN
WILL PAY FOR BTCV TO PLANT AND CARE FOR A TREE.

Contents

4   Monitors, standards and graphics cards   **59**

5   Ports   **76**

6   Setting up   **90**

Preface

The mass production of PC chips and circuit boards of all types has led to a thriving assembly industry in PC machines. In addition, various legal actions in the USA have allowed manufacturers other than Intel to produce chips that can be described as 166MMX or similar designations. The result is that it has for many years been possible for anyone with facilities for assembling circuit boards into cases to put together PCs with capabilities equal to all but a few modern designs. The sheer number of small-scale suppliers, and the standardization of design, indicates how easy this work can be, using plug-in boards from the lowest cost sources. Construction, in this sense, can mean assembly, and not necessarily much assembly in some examples.

- The small-scale assemblers, some of whom can offer 166MMX (or higher) machines with 32 Mbyte of memory for £600 or less, cannot offer much more than hardware. In particular, they cannot offer a manual that makes much sense to the first-time user, and even an experienced PC user can be baffled by a new machine if little or no information is available.

This book is a form of manual that will cover the construction of a PC, either from scratch or following the much more common (and more rational) method of buying a low-cost machine from a local assembler, or from other sources such as auctions, and improving it as required. This book will also be a useful reference text for users of all the machines that can be described as generic, machines which are very closely compatible with standard PC/AT design but with enhanced facilities. If your low-cost PC comes provided with a manual that can be politely described as rudimentary, this book is for you. Since it is assumed that you are building a new PC or updating an old one, information that is relevant only to very old machines is omitted unless you need to know it for the purposes of updating. The use of old machines (prior to the 80486 models) is a problem that makes many books on the PC machine bulkier than they need be just to account for all the variations that are required on older machines.

- To clarify terms, the first IBM desktop machines were known as PC, meaning personal computer. AT means Advanced Technology, and the PC/AT type of machine set the standard that is still followed (with improvements) today. This type of machine is also referred to as ISA, meaning Industry Standard Architecture, and the letters EISA (E meaning Extended or Enhanced) are also used of the later versions such as the MMX types.

One point that often worries prospective DIY builders is that their machine will be non-standard. The fact is that a home-constructed machine is likely to be totally standard, more so than some big-name varieties, and more adaptable to upgrading. Another worry is that some inadvertent action will destroy the whole machine, and this also is a myth unless you make a habit of dropping hammers into equipment. Perhaps we should add the worry that the machine will be damaged in some way by unsuitable software or when a program locks up. As this book points out, the computer clears its memory when it is switched off, and a fault in a program cannot affect any other program that is run after restarting like this. Unless a runaway program has, by a most unusual fluke, altered the contents of the hard drive, no harm will be done. By contrast, the type of program that we class as a virus will often alter the hard drive contents.

As it happens, building a PC from scratch is usually more expensive than buying a machine from some of the small-scale firms, and most private owners take the course of buying only as much as they need of an assembled machine – often a case, PSU, and mother-board only. Many suppliers specialize in this type of *bare-bones* machine, and because the parts are usually standardized, such machines are easy to work with and to upgrade. By starting in this way you can gain a price advantage, because there is no way that you can buy components cheaper than an assembler who can buy in bulk. The casing, for example, that costs you £55 may have been bought for less than £10 each, but only in container loads. You may, however, feel that you can use the monitor, casing, key-board and some other parts from an old machine that you are cur-rently using.

The point of assembling your PC in this way is that you can also upgrade for yourself, avoiding the high costs that are so often asso-ciated with changing hardware. A second-hand computer, after all, depreciates like a second-hand car. Apart from anything else, who wants a machine that will not be able to keep track of the date after midnight on 31 December 1999? Only a modern machine of the Pentium class (or later) can be guaranteed to avoid the problems associated with the change to the year 2000 (the last year of the twentieth Century) and thereafter.

Another route which is now significant is to buy machines that have been discarded by local authorities and other corporate users. The more a local authority or nationalized service complains about lack of money the more computers they appear to scrap (not sell), simply because they are not the most recent models. These machines are found at auctions and at car-boot sales, often at very low prices. Some are older 80486 types, others are almost new Pentium machines which have been used in networks and which may lack a hard drive. Prices of £50 to £100 make this a very encouraging start and one which is much cheaper than buying all parts separ-ately.

The aim of the book is to provide information for anyone taking any of these routes, because no manuals will be available. Since many readers of this book are likely to be experienced in electronics, some aspects of computer circuitry and disk recording are explained in more detail than would be relevant to the reader with no elec-tronics background. Other than these paragraphs, the book is intended to be used by newcomers and experienced users alike, either in computing or in electronics.

The book is divided roughly into three parts. Chapters 1 to 3 cover the work involved in creating your own computer from scratch, or from a few items that you already have. Chapters 4 to 8 are concerned with making improvements on a machine to bring it up to date, which will refer back to some topics covered earlier. The third part, Chapters 9 to 11, is a guide to closely associated items such as printers and Windows.

Finally, this book is also intended as a reference to anyone who is updating a machine, either a minor update such as replacing a disk drive, or a major update such as replacing a motherboard. Since the effects of construction and upgrading cannot be judged without the essential software, the essentials of using MS-DOS and Windows are also included, along with a chapter on printers.

Ian Sinclair

Chapter 1

Preliminaries, fundamentals and buying guide

The PC machine

This chapter, and the two that follow, are intended primarily for the prospective assembler of a PC whose experience has been in electronics construction rather than in computing. It is, however, also an essential guide to anyone who is constructing a PC with no previous electronics experience. If you are already well experienced in computing and want to experience the joys of self-assembly then read this by all means, but be prepared to skip some explanations that are intended for the newcomer to computers.

To start with, the type of machine that we now describe as a PC means one that is modelled on the IBM PC type of machine that first appeared in 1980. The reason that this type of machine has become dominant is the simple one of continuity – programs (*software applications*) that will work on the original IBM PC machine will work on later versions and will still work on today's Windows PC machines (using the MS-DOS window). By maintaining compatibility, the designers have ensured that when you change computer, keeping to a PC type of machine, you do not necessarily need to change software (programs). Since the value of your software is much greater than the value of the hardware (the computer itself), this has ensured that the PC type of machine became dominant in business and other serious applications. Other machines that are not compatible with the PC or with each other have less choice of software and more expensive components.

Compatibility works only one way, however, and most of the (Windows) software that is being written now will not run on older machines, though a lot of old-style MS-DOS programs still do. The main benefit of a long-established design is that components are remarkably cheap and reliable, and that the layout of machines is more or less standardized. Though you can build or buy an old-style machine for a low price, it is well worth the small amount of extra cash to construct or buy a PC machine that is reasonably up to date in design. This allows you the luxury of being able to use *any* software written for the PC, not just the older programs. You should aim for a machine that can run Windows 98, the current version of the Windows system (see Chapter 9). Another advantage of building a machine using modern hardware is that you can be certain it will not misbehave when the date changes from 1999 to 2000.

In short, a modern PC/AT machine is currently identified by the following points:

1. It uses a microprocessor which is an Intel Pentium or a compatible chip from AMD, Cyrix, IBM, IDT, or other manufacturer of this status.
2. It uses a program called MS-DOS or PC-DOS as a master controlling system (an operating system), to enable it to load and run all other programs.
3. It has enough hard drive and memory space to run Windows 98.

What and why?

Before you think of spending any hard-earned money on a PC machine you need to think carefully about what your needs are. Generally, when you buy a computer for the first time you have some main use in mind. This might be word processing because you need to write reports, articles, sermons, notes, books or whatever. It might be database use, because you need to keep track of several thousand items in a mail-order catalogue or points in a sports league or references in newspapers. It might be a spreadsheet because you need to keep tables of items in a way that allows you to work out totals and averages, or it might be a bookkeeping or accounting program for your business needs.

Whatever your needs are initially, once you have experienced the advantages of working with the computer, and adapted your methods to the use of the computer, you will want to make it work harder for you. You are likely to buy other main items of software, and you are also likely to want to use the programs that are collectively called *utilities*.

The point about adapting your methods is important. Any task that you have previously done by hand usually needs to be done quite differently by computer. The computer forces you to work in a different way, but as a compensation it allows you to work with greater freedom. You can make corrections and alterations easily, for example. Try typing an article and then inserting a 20-word amendment in the middle of the work. This is simple routine stuff when you use a word processor, tedious and awkward when you use a steam typewriter. Try using a card index to produce a list of all UNF-threaded bolts in size 6 with cadmium plating and hex heads – it's easy with the computer running a database, but you must have organized the information correctly in the first place, and not as you would for a card index. When users feel disappointed with the use of a computer, the reason is almost always that they are trying to make the machine work in the way that they formerly worked with pen and paper.

Whatever you bought the machine for in the first place, you are likely to find that you have many more applications for it after a year or so. This is when you may come up against restrictions that seemed unlikely when you first bought the machine. You may need more memory to run larger programs, more disk space to store them, faster actions, and a better monitor. If you chose wisely initially you should find that your machine is capable as it is, and even if you went for the minimum that you could get away with, wise planning will ensure that you can easily upgrade the machine to do what you want. That sort of action is also covered in this book. Remember, however, that upgrading a computer is rather like upgrading a HiFi system – it can be continued forever and eventually the gains are too small to notice. You have to ask yourself continually if an upgrade really fulfils a need or whether it simply allows you to use a more elaborate version of a program that serves you perfectly well at the moment.

- One problem that has been with us since small computers became available is *bloatware*. This means software that comes out in a new enhanced and much larger form each year. You have to decide for yourself when the software that you use provides you with all you need, and if a new version that is twice the size and runs at half the speed is really useful.
- Currently, upgrading is important, because the machines that were available before the Pentium chip became available may not be able to cope with the change of year from 1999 to 2000. There is free software available (on the Internet) to detect whether your computer can cope or not, and to diagnose whether it needs some software or a chip replacement. If you are building a new machine or replacing a motherboard on an old machine you should not need to worry about this problem, and the software you use should not be a problem unless you are using very old software. On average, software has a life of up to five years, so that only older software is likely to be suspect. My 1995 Accounts program, for example, is fully capable of operating beyond the year 2000.

Upgrading the machine is not confined to simply increasing its memory and its ability to deal with more complex programs. Add-on boards exist for virtually every purpose for which a computer can be adapted, and the PC machine forms an excellent basis for experimental work for anyone with experience in electronics. The current add-on fashion is fast video boards, allowing you to edit your camcorder tapes or work on video images from TV or from a video recorder. Similarly, you can capture Teletext pages, compensating for the short-sighted design of TV receivers that makes no provision for attaching a printer. You can also use your PC along with a digital camera and colour printer to replace the tedious business of buying films that have to be developed and printed, with no editing facilities.

A less-trumpeted aspect is control engineering, using analogue–digital converter cards, allowing the PC to act as part of a control system for process engineering, environmental control and so on. Similar add-on cards can also be used to make the PC part of a security system with the advantage that the response can be altered by programming the machine for yourself. You can also couple in devices such as bar-code readers and printers to make the PC part of a data system. All of these actions are too specialized for this book, but you should be aware that they exist and if you are interested, look out for books that deal with these topics. For some of these actions you do not need the latest and fastest type of PC, and in some cases the requirements are very modest.

The components

A basic PC system consists of a main casing that contains the power supply in a sealed box, the motherboard and the disk drives, along with a separate keyboard and monitor. The keyboard and the contents of the main casing are the components that lend themselves to DIY assembly, and the monitor is bought as a single, separate, item. A modern monitor will be a 15″ or 17″ colour unit capable of much higher resolution than a TV receiver (and costing quite a lot more).

The main advice here is to avoid working with the older components. The 8088, 8086, 80286 and 80386 microprocessors are now completely obsolete and though there are millions of PCs working happily with these processors, they are not capable of running the mainstream of modern programs, particularly Windows 95 and 98. Even the comparatively recent 80486 is by now too restricted in speed to run modern software. Windows 98 needs a machine which is initially as capable as you can afford, and which can easily be upgraded, particularly with more memory, later. You will handicap yourself if you build using the old components unless you are simply practising for a later effort.

The assembly of a PC machine from scratch is, if anything, easier than making a working model from old-style Meccano, with the difference that you start with a full kit of bigger parts. The comparison is not entirely fanciful either, because a PC is put together using bolts of standard types, and circuit boards that plug into position; no elaborate tools are required or vast experience needed. What you need to know is what parts you need, where to buy them and how to put them together. You do *not* need to know how to solder, and the highest order of electrical work you will be called on to do will be to connect up a standard mains plug.

The tools you need are mainly screwdrivers, preferably in the smaller sizes, and both plain and cross-head types. A pair of pliers is also useful though seldom essential, and tweezers are useful for retrieving small bolts from inaccessible places. Other than these you need common sense (square plugs do not go into round holes) and some motivation (such as lack of money or fascination with computers). One useful point about assembling your own PC is that you can do it step by step. If cash is limited, you can buy one part each month until you complete the assembly.

On the subject of cost, assembling a PC from scratch is always going to be more costly than buying a new machine made from the same parts and bought from the cheapest sources after some shopping around. The lowest-cost suppliers are almost always going to be small-scale mail-order suppliers or stall-holders at computer fairs and because they work on lower margins than the others they are more vulnerable to problems like slow payers, worried banks and strikes in delivery services. Because of this, you should always assume that such a supplier is unlikely to be a permanent fixture, and you should not part with real money. If you pay using a credit card (either in person or over the telephone) you have the protection of the credit card company. If the supplier vanishes overnight you will not lose because your card account will not be debited. There is no other way of paying that is so secure.

- Remember that mail-order suppliers will usually add a charge for courier delivery that will put anything from £6 to £10 on to your costs (and with VAT over and above). You can avoid these costs if you can buy at a computer fair or from a local assembler.
- You do not need to build from scratch, however. You can use the casing and power supply from an old machine or buy a package of parts that will start you off at a lower price than you would pay if you bought each part individually.

Looking for suppliers is easy if you subscribe to magazines such as *PC Shopper*, whose advertisers include many that specialize in parts for the DIY assembler. Do not confine yourself to these, however, because shopping around is important, and you may find bargains from suppliers who make no claims to cater for the assembler but who nevertheless hold an immense stock of PC parts at low prices.

BUILD AND UPGRADE YOUR OWN PC

A few hours spent with these magazines can save you a lot of hard-earned cash because you learn what the going price is for everything.

All of this refers to standard desktop machines. Portable computers are quite another thing because there is no standard design, the parts are costly and difficult to obtain, and you need a ten-year apprenticeship as a sardine-packer to be able to work on them. There are many buyers of portable machines, but fewer serious users who would not be as well served with a notebook and a pencil. Oddly enough, quite a few people have told me that they would like a portable that could be used simply to make notes that could be transcribed to a PC later. Such a machine would have a decent-sized keyboard, a floppy drive, software in ROM, and cost under £200. I often wonder why there isn't one – the nearest we ever got to this ideal was the Amstrad NC200.

The essential bits

The essential main bits of a PC are the casing (with power supply), the motherboard, video card, and the disk drives. To check that a machine is working you also need a monitor, but since this is bought ready-made and can outlast several computers we do not count it, or a printer, as part of a DIY project. Do *not* attempt to convert a TV receiver into a monitor, or convert an old monitor into something suited to a modern PC, unless you have considerable experience of working on TV equipment.

● Note in particular that any monitor *must* use an earthed chassis, and if you intend to work on a monitor you must have suitable circuit diagrams. The reasons for this are noted in Chapter 4.

Monitors from other types of machines will not necessarily be suited to a PC computer, though a few are adaptable. Be particularly careful of monitors, particularly large-screen monitors, offered as bargains. Some of these work with non-standard graphics boards which must be supplied along with the monitor, because they cannot be connected to a standard VGA board, but you cannot be sure that your software will be able to use such a monitor correctly, if at all.

With the essential bits in hand you can connect up a working PC machine in under an hour, though it will not necessarily do everything that you want. From that stage, however, you can add other facilities by plugging in additional circuit boards, called expansion cards, to extend the capabilities of the machine. You can also plug in additional memory units (called SIMMs), because whatever you do with a machine is likely to require more memory sooner or later unless you start with as much memory as the motherboard can take. At the time of writing, memory is not expensive but don't buy until you really need to.

The motherboard, as the name suggests, is the main printed circuit board of any PC machine which carries any other boards (or *cards*) that are added. It is a multi-layer board, and you must never drill it or cut it because the tracks that you see on it are only the surface tracks with others hidden between layers. The motherboard contains the main microprocessor chip (the CPU), and the type of CPU that is used determines the performance of the computer. At the time of writing, low-cost motherboards use the Intel Pentium 166MMX or an equivalent made by other suppliers such as AMD, Cyrix, IDT or IBM. The older chips are graded by number, and you should not consider using a motherboard, no matter how cheap to buy, with a CPU whose number indicates an earlier design, such as the 80486, 80386, 80286, 8086 or 8088.

- The important point of buying a modern motherboard intended for the 166MMX type of chip is that the chip is held in a socket called Socket-7. This allows you to replace the 166 chip by faster units (200, 233, 266) if you need more speed. The more expensive boards that use the special socket for the Pentium-II chip are not ideal for your purposes. If you find from studying magazines that the Socket-7 is becoming obsolete and that all chip suppliers are moving to the other design then it will be time to think again.

The Intel chips are all currently called Pentium – a name was used because a name can be patented, unlike a number. No supplier other than Intel can offer a Pentium chip (unless licensed by Intel), but you will find other chips that are compatible with the Pentium. At present, Intel markets a Pentium-II chip that uses a different type of socket compared to the first Pentium version. A new (cut-down) version of this chip is being marketed under the name Celerix. Whatever may happen in the future, it is likely that if you have not felt a pressing need for a computer up until now you certainly don't need to use a chip that is at the forefront of technology. The older Pentium MMX types, using the Socket-7 connector, are capable of much more than 99% of its users require. Though it is now regarded by Intel as older technology, this is the one to go for at the moment because it is readily available, low priced, reliable, and likely to be around for a considerable time. After all, the 8088 was being supplied in new machines for 12 years. The equivalents of the 200MMX chip from other manufacturers include the AMD K6X86-PR200, Cyrix M2-200+, IBM PR200MMX, and new IDT 200MMX Winchip. The Winchip is not, strictly speaking, an exact equivalent and can be slower in action on some types of software, notably CAD.

As well as the main CPU and the sockets for memory SIMMs, the motherboard contains all the other supporting chips and the connections (or *bus*) between the CPU and other sections. The other notable feature of the motherboard is the provision of *slots*, sockets for cards that are plugged in to expand the use of the machine. There are two different types of slots, called ISA and PCI respectively, and a good motherboard should allow three or more of each type of slot. These are considered in more detail in Chapter 2.

- If you are offered a board with the VLB type of bus, decline politely. This was an older type of bus used on 80486 machines but rapidly replaced by the PCI type of bus. You should also avoid boards that use the MCA type of bus that was also a short-lived form of bus used mainly on IBM machines.

A microprocessor that fits Socket-7 is a component that you can replace easily if you want to upgrade, because the socket uses a clamping system called ZIF (zero insertion force). You remove the cooling fan, pull out a lever on the socket and move it through 90°, and this releases the chip which can easily be lifted out. The new chip is then dropped into the socket, and the lever replaced to lock it in place. You need only clip on the cooling fan and connect it up.

- A fan costs around £10 if bought separately, but you will usually get a fan along with a processor. There are two types. One type takes its power from the disk drive supplies, the other type from a set of pins on the motherboard. The first type can be fitted on any machine, but the second can be used only if the power supply pins are on the motherboard. The second type is better if you want to make use of the chip temperature monitoring features of a modern motherboard.

When you want to upgrade a computer that uses a chip of pre-Pentium type, very often soldered into place, the simple and sensible method is to replace the whole motherboard. You might be able to transfer the memory SIMMs from the old board to the new one, but it's most unlikely that the old machine had enough memory or that the SIMMs were of the modern type. You can transfer the ISA slot cards, if you need them, with rather more certainty. That way you take advantage of not only the new microprocessor, but improvements in motherboard design as well.

The casing contains the power supply for the PC, which is always the type referred to as *switch-mode*, along with space for the motherboard, a set of shelves, called *bays*, for disk drives, various LED indicators and switches, and a lot of empty space. The most useful type of casing is also the cheapest and uses a hinged lid or a small (mini or midi) tower construction. Do not be tempted by miniature slimline cases or tall full-size tower-block types, because they are more expensive and often difficult to work with if you want to add more disk drives and cards.

- Casings now come in two types as well as a variety of shapes and sizes. The fundamental types are Baby AT and ATX. The Baby AT cases are still in the majority, but this may not last for long. The ATX cases use a different motherboard layout and a different power supply plug, and though you can put a modern Baby AT board into an ATX casing, you cannot put an ATX motherboard into a Baby AT casing.

The side or front of the casing contains an opening for the main switch of the power supply unit, and the back right-hand side of the casing also has a set of six or more openings, usually temporarily covered by metal strips. These openings are at the slot positions, and each time you expand the capabilities of the computer by adding a card, it is likely that one cover plate will have to be removed to allow a connector mounted on the card to project outside the casing. These metal strips are each located by a single screw, usually of the cross-head variety. Do not use the machine with strips removed unless there are connectors to replace them, because this will upset the fan-driven airflow inside the machine. The front panel of the casing has cut-outs for CD and disk drives, and also a panel of switches and LEDs.

The disk and CD drives are the other essentials, because a computer by itself is as useless as a CD player with no CDs. In computer jargon, the hardware is useless without software. Most of the memory of a computer is the kind described as *volatile*, meaning that it is wiped clear each time the machine is switched off, so that all the instruction codes that the machine needs to do anything have to be stored in a more permanent form. The three most familiar permanent forms are as a chip (a ROM or read-only memory chip), a magnetized disk, or a CD drive. Modern machines use all three of these systems, and your motherboard will contain one or more ROM chips that contain a comparatively small amount of code. This is sufficient only to allow the machine to respond to the keyboard (in a limited way) and to operate the disk drive(s), also in a limited way. The rest of the essential codes, the operating system, are read in (loaded) from a disk.

- The ROM, also called the BIOS, incidentally, is the part that has to be replaced in older machines that does not recognize the year 2000. If you buy a new, modern motherboard you will not need to worry about year 2000 problems. Incidentally, because our calendar starts at year AD 1 and the previous year was 1 BC, the first year of the second millenium is 2001, as Arthur C. Clark recognized in the title of his book. The idea of a year zero was not around two thousand years ago.

The aim of this multi-part storage is to build into the machine just sufficient permanent instructions to read in an operating system that you can choose for yourself. The operating system is something that needs to be upgraded each time the capabilities of the computer are extended and if it were in ROM form it would require the ROM chips to be replaced. This action of using a small section of code to read in the rest of the operating codes is called bootstrapping (from the old myth of lifting yourself by your own bootstraps) or *booting*, and the action of switching on a computer is referred to as *booting up*. The smallest portable machines do not use a disk drive, and they keep all of their operating system code in a ROM.

The main ROM chip is called the BIOS, meaning Basic Input Output Services, and this is a good description of what it provides.

BIOS chips can come from a variety of suppliers, and the type that you find on your motherboard determines what additional facilities you may be able to call on. In particular, the BIOS chip controls a small CMOS RAM memory chip that is used to store machine information such as the date and the machine facilities, using a battery backup so that the information is held permanently (as long as the battery lasts) but can be changed at will.

The disk drives are vital to a desktop machine, and all modern machines need at least three – one floppy drive that uses replaceable magnetic disks, one hard drive which uses a set of disks that are fixed and encased in a sealed container, and a CD-ROM drive. The floppy drive is used so that you can copy short programs (software) that you buy and place on the hard drive, and also for holding your own data. A hard drive has a limited life, so that it is essential to have a copy on tape, on floppy disks or on CD-ROM of everything on the hard drive. At one time it was possible to use a computer with a floppy drive only, but modern programs are too large to fit on a floppy drive, and the drive itself is too slow to allow a program to be run using just the floppy drive. The CD drive is used because the size of modern software is just too much to allow the economical use of floppy disks, and some machines now come with CD drives that allow writing a CD as well as reading it.

The motherboard carries the disk interface circuits which convert the numbers stored in the memory into pulses that can be recorded magnetically, and vice versa. The type of disk interface that is almost universally used at the time of writing is the ATA or EIDE system, the initials meaning AT Attachment and Extended Integrated Drive Electronics respectively. You will find two sockets on the motherboard labelled as Primary and Secondary IDE connectors respectively, and the usual arrangement is to connect the hard drive to the Primary IDE and the CD-ROM drive to the Secondary IDE connector. On older computers, these sockets were not on the motherboard and had to be added by way of a card plugged into a slot.

- The term ATA has appeared more recently to mean what we all used to call IDE. The reason for the distinction is that this is the more correct name, because SCSI drives (see later) are, technically, also integrated drive types and could be termed IDE.

The card that usually has to be added (into a PCI type of slot) is the video graphics card that converts the computer pulses into video signals that a monitor can use. Once again there is a universal standard called VGA or SVGA, and adding this card will allow you to connect up the monitor and see what happens when the computer is switched on. The video card should be of the PCI type, and nowadays should contain some 2 Mbyte or more of memory. What happens from that point onwards depends on the software which is the subject of later chapters in this book. Because changing a graphics card is often an upgrading action, it has also been placed in a later chapter.

- The assembly of casing, with power supply, the motherboard loaded with memory, and the disk drives plus video card, keyboard and monitor constitute a working computer.

Finally in this introduction, computing has enriched the English language with a large number of new words and new uses of old words. If these are new to you, Appendix A contains a glossary with full explanations, and some have been explained already in this chapter. Note that the word disk is used to refer to a magnetic computer disc, and the more familiar *disc* is used for CDs. This distinction has become important now that the CD format is used to distribute software, replacing the use of floppy disks.

Chapter 2

Case, motherboard and keyboard

The casing of a computer is its most obvious hardware aspect, often labelled as boring by people who should know better (if you want bright transfers you can apply them yourself). A full-scale desktop casing is around 14″ wide by 16″ deep by 6.5″ high, but there are many other varieties of various descriptions such as small-footprint, minicase and so on. The full size of case was needed in the early days when the main board (motherboard) was large and when a small disk drive implied a 5.25″ full-height unit. Nowadays, slimmer casings can be used, and often are because motherboards are smaller and disk drives are slimmer. Many manufacturers now use a tower-block form of casing in which the casing rests on its 14″ × 6.5″ side. In the tower class you will find mini, midi and full-size towers. The full-sized tower should be used only for server machines that need a large number of disk drives (usually seven or more).

The casing is not just something that should concern you if you are building a machine for yourself. The casing that a manufacturer has used for a machine determines quite critically what you can do in the way of adding new facilities and replacing the motherboard. Since a computer design can be considered as fairly new for only a few months, it is important to be able to upgrade a machine easily. Even if you are starting with buying a machine that is, by modern standards, obsolete, you should not neglect the case design, because it may make the difference between being able to upgrade cheaply by replacing a motherboard or expensively by having to replace everything. The quality of the case is often the best way of deciding between two clones of unknown name and almost identical appearance. No matter how neat and tidy a small casing may look, it is not necessarily something that you will congratulate yourself about later.

- The first big decision when you are starting from scratch is whether to buy the classic Baby AT casing or the later ATX. *You should always go for the ATX design.* The layout is better, with better cooling and interior layout, and though you can fit a modern Baby AT motherboard into an ATX casing, you cannot fit a new ATX motherboard into the older type of Baby AT casing. The slightly higher price of the ATX casing gives you some degree of future-proofing, because this type of case will eventually be the only type supplied.
- Another important point is that if you move later to a Pentium-II type of motherboard this will be of the ATX type requiring an ATX casing.

What should you look for in a casing? A metal casing is important, because a metal casing greatly reduces the radiation of radio interference from the computer. Some big-name manufacturers in the past have used plastic cases and been obliged also to use metal sheets internally to comply with radio interference regulations. You should not attempt to upgrade a machine by using a case of this type. Using a metal case is a much easier solution, and the best form of case for easy working is the established flip-lid type which allows easy access to the interior simply by pressing two catches and lifting the lid up on its hinges. Plastic casings are not on offer for self-assembly, so if you are starting from scratch you will quite certainly be buying a steel casing. Figure 2.1 shows examples of a desktop and a tower casing of a type ideal for the constructor.

The overall size is not quite so important as the space for internal components, and one of the most important of these considerations is the number of disk drive bays. A disk drive bay, Figure 2.2, of the older conventional sort is a shelf which is intended for the older type of 5.25″ disk drive, and is used nowadays for the CD-ROM drive. Such a drive will slide into the bay from the front and be

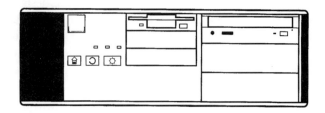

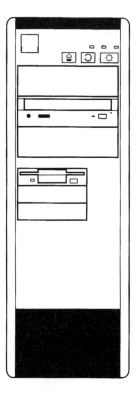

2.1 Examples of case shapes, desktop and midi-tower.

secured by screws at the side of the bay. The piece of casing at the front of the bay is usually a clip-on plastic portion which can be discarded when a floppy disk drive is fitted into the bay. A good case should offer *at least* two such bays, and *at least* two other smaller bays that will take a 3.5″ drive – one will be used for a hard disk drive and the other for the main floppy drive. There may be one or more 3.5″ bays with no front panels that can be used for hard drives.

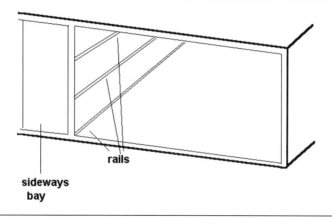

2.2 Typical 5.25″ bays as seen from the front of a flip-lid casing.

The importance of drive bays cannot be over-estimated. You might think that one 5.25″ bay would be enough, but items such as tape backup drives and read/write CD drives need this size of bay, and there may be many other add-ons that are under development that will require these fittings. If your case is lacking in drive bays and you need more drives then you will have a buy a larger case and start again. The only other option is to add new drives externally until the next time you rebuild.

● Another important point is that if you buy a larger casing, the power supply within it usually provides more connectors. This also is important if you are likely to add other drives.

The older type of large casing looks very empty when the lid is raised, because modern motherboards are so much smaller than their predecessors. This makes more room for clipping other accessories, and it is not an advantage, as noted above, to opt for a small case unless you are very short of desk space. The conventional setup of a PC machine is to use the flip-lid case to support the monitor, with the keyboard in front of both. The cables that are supplied will usually allow for other configurations – for example, I have the main cases for two machines on a shelf under the desk, with only the monitors and the keyboards on top. This confers the advantage that I can look downwards at the monitors without needing to jack up the chair to an unreasonable height. A tower form of casing also allows for more versatility in placing the units.

The back of the casing should allow for at least as many slot openings as the motherboard uses, or, if possible, more. The number of the slots on the motherboard governs the number of add-on boards that can be used, and though you can easily estimate how many you need now, it is less easy to guess how many more you might want in a few months' time. The number of slot positions in the casing determines how many boards can be used along with connectors that protrude from the back of the casing, and though several boards do not need connectors, it is always advisable to assume that each board will need to have a connector. On modern machines the demand for slots is less because the disk interfaces are built into the motherboard, and on some motherboards the video circuits and the sound card are also built in. Because of this you may find new motherboards with very few slots provided, mainly PCI slots.

The hardware that comes attached to the casing is also worth looking at. There will always be an on/off switch and often a reset switch. The reset switch is almost always at the front of the casing, and most users would prefer it to be at the back, well out of the way of fingers to avoid being pressed accidentally. There should also be LED indicators for power on and, usually, another to indicate when the hard disk is reading or writing. The leads that are connected to these switches and LEDs are fairly well standardized. Older case designs provided for a turbo switch and indicator, and sometimes a keylock switch; these are not needed now.

The small loudspeaker which is used to provide warning notes is built into the case, and provided with leads that should reach the corresponding connectors on the motherboard. The location of the loudspeaker is not fixed, and different manufacturers are likely to place this component in different positions, but usually near the front of the case. The loudspeaker is of portable-radio standard, and is used only for warning beeps. Provision for sound on modern machines is made by way of a separate sound card with external loudspeakers.

The case should provide an opening for the main ON/OFF switch which is part of the power supply box. This sometimes protrudes through the slot at the rear right-hand side of the casing and because the maker of the case cannot know what make of power supply will be fitted, you may find that the switch is a tight fit. If you come across this problem you can either slightly adjust the power supply position, or enlarge the slot in the case so as to free the switch. If you need to file the slot edges, make sure that all metal filings are removed before you fit anything else to the casing. Modern cases usually place the power switch at the front, connected to the power supply box by a cable.

Finally, the floor of the casing has pillars that will support a motherboard. Very often there are more pillars than the motherboard needs, and there may be some mounting holes on the motherboard that do not correspond to pillar positions. This is seldom a problem, because provided the motherboard is well supported it does not need to be bolted down in many places.

The motherboard

The motherboard, Figure 2.3, is the main board that contains the microprocessor, its support chips and the main system memory. This illustration shows the outline of the Baby AT type of motherboard, see below. Early motherboards were large because the memory, up to 640 Kbyte in those days, consisted of a large number (typically 18 or 36) of individual memory chips, each with a comparatively small amount of memory. For some time in the late 1980s and early 1990s, motherboards were supplied with 1 Mbyte of memory in this chip format with provision for adding more memory by inserting SIMM or SIPP assemblies. Figure 2.4 shows the shape of a modern ATX motherboard. These board outlines are not to scale.

- The slots on the motherboard always face to the rear of the computer, and the keyboard connector must also be at the rear, but otherwise the position of components is not fixed, nor are the precise dimensions.
- Modern motherboards almost all conform to either the Baby AT pattern or the more recent ATX design. The ATX type of motherboard *must* be put into an ATX type of case, but you can put a Baby AT board into most types of ATX cases. If you are building from scratch you should certainly go for the ATX motherboard and case. Avoid any motherboard that is not of one

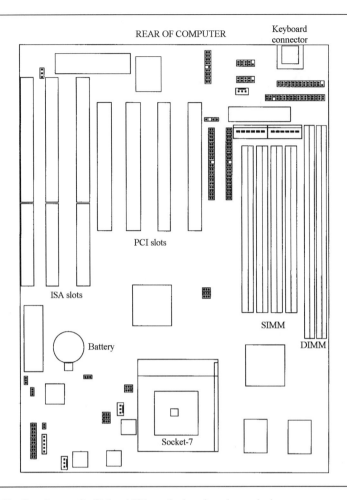

REAR OF COMPUTER

Keyboard connector

PCI slots

ISA slots

SIMM

DIMM

Battery

Socket-7

2.3 Outline shape of a Baby AT board, showing the main items.

of these types. Some 'famous-name' machines use motherboards that are totally incompatible, so that their casings are unusable for normal motherboards.

SIMM memory, an acronym of Single In-line Memory Module, uses a strip of high-capacity memory chips, usually three chips, in a slim card unit, Figure 2.5. The SIMM makes contact with the motherboard through a set of thin metal strips which are inserted into a SIMM socket on the motherboard. The normal method of fitting nowadays is to slide the strip into its holder tilted at 45°, and

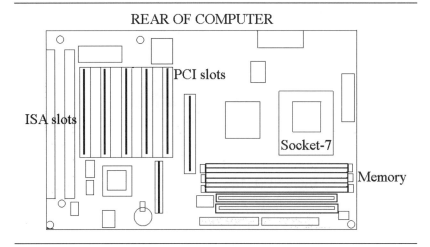

ISA slots

PCI slots

Socket-7

Memory

2.4 Outline shape of an ATX board, showing the main items.

then secure it by turning the unit until it is at right angles to the motherboard, Figure 2.6. This locks the SIMM in place and ensures that all the contacts are made securely.

SIMM exists in several forms. The older 30-pin type is obsolete, and all modern SIMMs use a 72-pin connection. The older variety is seldom used now, and the current hot favourite is the EDO SIMM, EDO meaning Extended Data Out. At the time of writing, several improved designs are in competition, and you should always use the type of memory modules that are recommended in the motherboard manual. For all Pentium machines, SIMMs need to be installed in pairs, one pair forming a bank of memory. If you

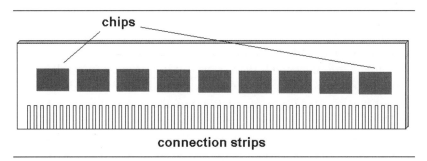

chips

connection strips

2.5 A SIMM board. This is an older type using nine chips.

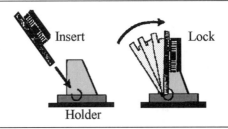

Insert   Lock

Holder

2.6 How the SIMM board is inserted and locked into place.

use a pair of 8 Mbyte SIMMs, for example, this gives a 16 Mbyte memory, which is about the minimum you can get away with these days.

● Some older machines use quite small-capacity SIMMs, but use all the SIMM sockets, so that 16 Mbyte of memory is achieved using 4×4 Mbyte SIMMs. Nowadays it would be more usual to supply a 16 Mbyte machine with 2×8 Mbyte SIMMs, allowing you to expand with another pair (perhaps 2×8 Mbyte, or 2×16 Mbyte).

Most modern motherboards will also cater for DIMM memory units, a type of double SIMM with 168 pins. These *can* be used singly, but each different type of motherboard has its own rules for using memory, and you may find that you cannot mix SIMM and DIMM, or that the DIMM has to be put into a designated holder if SIMM is present. Once again, you have to check this out from the motherboard manual, which will also advise on the use of the most recent memory types that can be used. At the time of writing, new forms of memory boards were appearing at frequent intervals.

● Whatever may happen in the design of memory units, your motherboard will be able to cater only for the units that were available at the time of manufacture. This makes it important to go for a motherboard that is as up to date as possible. You should also try to leave space for additional memory – do not, for example, fit 16 Mbyte of memory in the form of four 4 Mbyte SIMMs when you could at no more cost use two 8 Mbyte SIMMs. Nowadays it would be more normal to fit two 16 Mbyte SIMMs to give 32 Mbyte, allowing for expansion to 64 Mbyte or more later.

BUILD AND UPGRADE YOUR OWN PC

SLOTS

The slots on the motherboard, illustrated in Figures 2.3 and 2.4, are the connectors that hold and make connection to expansion boards. This follows the system used on the original PC machine and featured even earlier on the Apple computers of the late 1970s.

On current motherboards, two, three, or four slots will be the ISA type, the familiar type of expansion slot used in PC/AT computers for many years. Another three or four will be the more recent PCI type, using a smaller connector and 142 pins for the PCI local bus. This type of slot is used for expansion cards that must run fast, such as graphics and video cards, and you can now buy other cards, even sound cards, that use this type of slot. For the sake of future-proofing you should use PCI cards where possible, and ISA only for non-essential purposes. At the time of writing, internal modems still use ISA connections, but many other cards use the PCI connection. Avoid cards that use the older type of local bus called VLB.

On a machine bought in *bare-bones* trim, you may find that only one of the PCI slots will be occupied, usually by a video card, and one ISA slot will be occupied by a sound card. Some motherboards supply one combined slot that will take either PCI or a more specialized type of connection. All of the motherboard slots are in positions that correspond to openings in the casing at the rear, Figure 2.7, which are normally covered.

The ISA expansion slots operate under a handicap that has been inherited from the original PC machine. Whatever the clock rate used by the processor on the motherboard, the clock rate on the ISA slots is much slower, as low as 4.16 MHz on old PC (XT) machines, though 8 MHz is used on later AT expansion slots. At one time this could be justified on the grounds that expansion cards

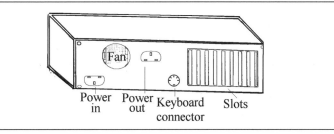

2.7 The rear of a flip-lid casing, showing the slots and connectors.

carried out actions that did not need a higher clock rate, and certainly this is true of such actions as parallel or serial ports, floppy drives and the older forms of graphics cards. The slow clock rate on the expansion slots is now a disadvantage for fast graphics cards. This is where local bus slots come in. A PCI local bus slot uses a much higher clock rate than the other slots, and can operate suitable cards at a more advantageous speed and with 32-bit data handling. Some motherboards contain a fast slot for graphics boards; these are called AGP slots

The need for slots arises from the need for expansion. If you want to add an optical read/write drive, a scanner, a tape backup or any of a host of desirable add-ons, each one is likely to require slot space for its controller. Once you have filled all of the slots your expansion capabilities are sharply brought to an end, because there is no easy way of providing for further expansion. Your only option then is to use expansion systems that act through the parallel port, using an adapter which still allows the printer to be used. This is not always a feasible scheme, because parallel ports on the older machines are strictly one way, and only a two-way parallel port can be used for this type of expansion for external drives. In addition, devices which connect to the parallel port in this way are often more expensive than those which simply slot in internally.

Power supply

The power supply unit (PSU) is the large box situated at the right-hand rear side of the computer (for a Baby AT casing), Figure 2.8, and prominently marked with notices that it must not be opened by unqualified personnel. Observe this warning, and, if you must open the box, first make certain that the machine is unplugged from the mains, that all cables have been disconnected, and that it has been switched off for at least ten minutes to allow capacitors to discharge.

The power supply box carries also the main switch and the casing fan, and it is connected (in the UK) by a standard three-pin rectangular socket of the type known as a Euroconnector. The plug end of this will be attached to a cable to which you can fit or have fitted a standard three-pin mains plug. The mains plug should carry a 3 A fuse – do not on any account use a larger rating.

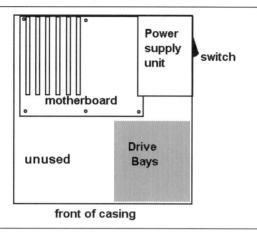

2.8 A typical Baby AT layout, showing the PSU position.

Power supplies are, almost universally, rated at 200 W. On the Baby AT type this provides for a 5 V supply at 25 amps, with +12 V, 5 amps and −12 V and −5 V at 1 amp each. This should be adequate for even the most heavily extended machine and for most users is much more than is needed, but the techniques that are used allow a 200 W unit to be built at virtually the same price of the older 150 W or 90 W types. The ATX power supply provides also 3.3 V supplies for modern processors and memory units, and uses a 20-pin plug, though most ATX units also provide the two 6-pin type of plugs that fit the Baby AT type of motherboard.

- One point to watch is the number of power supply plugs for drives. Many PSUs allow for only four of these, and this limits you to a floppy drive, a hard drive, a CD-ROM drive and one other. This is likely to be a bottleneck for expansion, because you may want to fit tape backup, a CD-RW drive and others that are at present in the development stage.
- If you have some experience of power supply units on other electronic equipment, note that the computer power units are of the switching type, and specialized knowledge is needed to deal with them if trouble arises. The one servicing exception is replacement of the main reservoir capacitor − this is usually the culprit if the unit fails after being switched off and on again several times in quick succession.

CASE, MOTHERBOARD AND KEYBOARD 25

The power supply incorporates its own fan, and there will be another fan fitted over the processor chip. This can be powered from a socket on the motherboard or it can use one of the supply connectors that is provided for disk drives. Most designs are over-generous with these connectors, and if the fan is powered in this way the adaptor that is provided will allow for connection to a disk drive if needed.

The power supply unit almost always includes an AC mains output, a 240 V mains supply which is controlled by the computer's main switch and available at a Eurosocket. This is normally used either for the monitor or the printer (it can be used for both if you can wire them appropriately). The output comes from a fixed socket, and a matching plug is seldom supplied. Few electrical shops stock such plugs, and they are best obtained by mail order, using firms such as ElectroMail or Maplin. The ElectroMail reference number for a suitable straight plug is 489-251 and the Maplin code is HL16S. Business users with an RS Components account can order using the same code as for ElectroMail.

Keyboards

The modern type of keyboard has 102 keys, laid out (Figure 2.9) in logical groupings. The function keys are set across the top of the keyboard, with the Esc key isolated to the left. The cursor movement keys are separated from the number keypad, as also are the Insert, Home Page Up, Page Down, Delete and End keys. The Ctrl keys are duplicated so that they can be used with either hand, making it easier to press Ctrl with any other key.

What you regard as a good keyboard is very much an individual preference. Most users like a keyboard to have a positive click action to the keys, but without excessive noise, and keyboards of the rubbery variety are universally disliked. IBM keyboards are very highly regarded by typists. Most anonymous keyboards are of a reasonable standard, and those branded with the name Cherry are highly regarded. Figure 2.10 shows a Maplin keyboard whose action is of the Cherry type, with a good response from the keys – they feel right, as opposed to the dead feel of some keyboards. Since

function keys

main keyboard / **cursor keys** / numeric keypad

ENTER key

2.9 A standard type of keyboard. Some later types add three more keys on the spacebar level to carry out Windows 95/98 actions.

the keyboard is your main communication with the computer, a good keyboard is important.

Though keyboards of the 102-key variety all look very similar, there are subtle differences. Some nameless clone machines come with US keyboards, which are easily detected because of the absence of the £ symbol (on the upper 3 key). Though a US keyboard can be used without difficulty, the absence of the £ sign can be irritat-

2.10 A photograph of a Maplin keyboard.

ing, though you can usually get the symbol by holding down the Alt key and typing the number 156 on the separate keypad, then releasing the Alt key. An alternative is the use of Windows Character Map. If you seldom need to use a £ sign, there is no problem.

- The Euro symbol, €, can be obtained by downloading a font called Euro collections from a Web site in Holland, www.xs4all.nl. Look for the file euro13tt.zip which can be downloaded and unpacked (using WinZip or other zip utility) to give the TTF TrueType font that you can add in to your Windows fonts. When the time comes (as it must, since politicians always get their own way) you can use the £ key to provide the € symbol instead.

A point that often causes confusion is the provision of an Alt key on the left of the spacebar and a key marked Alt Gr on the right-hand side. The Alt Gr key is intended to be used on machines that make use of the German character set and a lot of PC software will allow you to make use of either the Alt or Alt Gr key interchangeably. This is not always true, however. If you are accustomed to switching between Windows programs by using the Alt and Tab keys together you will find that the Alt Gr key cannot be substituted for the Alt key. Microsoft Word for Windows also ignores the Alt Gr key (and also the right-hand Ctrl key) for many of its actions. The main use of this Alt Gr key is to provide the third character on keys that display more than two character symbols. On UK keyboards the only character of this kind is the split bar ¦ which is usually shown also on the sloping front of the key next to the number 1 on the top row. One curious effect is that the solid bar and the split bar key symbols usually appear the other way around on the screen.

Keyboards should be kept covered when not in use, because dust can gather at an alarming rate. This can cause keys to jam, and when this happens you will see an error message appear when you try to boot up the machine. The message is 'Keyboard error' followed by a code number which shows which key is causing the error; for example, 0E indicates that the Alt key is jammed down.

Another factor to consider is how keyboards age. Some keyboards do not change at all in the course of their life, others alter quite noticeably. One of my keyboards (a US layout) started life with a pleasant click action, but has deteriorated so that keys now stick closed or jam open at times. The other keyboard has remained good, and an old Amstrad keyboard (pensioned off after four years and a million words typed) remains as good as new.

Never be tempted to spray WD40 or any other silicone lubricant onto a keyboard whose keys have started to become sticky. Using a spray virtually guarantees that some of the liquid, which is one of the best insulators known, will get into contacts, ensuring that the keyboard will never work again. You might be able to release one sticky key by careful lubrication using a drop of silicone oil on a piece of wire, but don't depend on it.

Motherboard preparation

Before you can consider starting assembly, the motherboard needs to be inspected carefully, and you also need to read the manual or other documents that accompany it. If there is no form of documentation, contact the suppliers of the motherboard because you cannot assume that you will be able to find the correct connections or to make the correct settings by instinct or by comparing it with an older motherboard.

Jumpers, Figure 2.11, are used to make contacts on the motherboard to switch actions in or out, or to allow for options. Each jumper unit normally consists of a row of three small pins with a bridging clip, the jumper itself, which can be placed over two pins to provide two settings (sometimes three settings if the design pro-

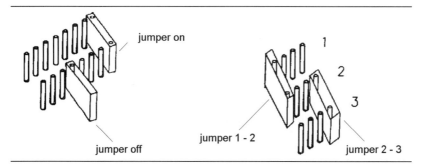

2.11 Jumpers and how they are used. Some modern motherboards completely dispense with the use of jumpers.

vides for the jumper to be removed altogether). Jumper settings should be correct if you have bought a bare-bones system with the motherboard already been installed in its case, and very often there is little chance of altering jumpers once the machine is fully assembled. A few motherboard designs are self-adjusting, so that no jumpers are provided.

If you are installing a new motherboard or replacing a motherboard, however, you will need to check the jumper settings very carefully before you place the new motherboard into the case. The small (and usually anonymous) manual or leaflet that comes with the motherboard will list the jumper settings, and these are usually preset correctly. If they are not, it is not always clear what settings you ought to use, and you may need to enquire from the supplier of the board. Another problem is that manuals usually show the pins numbered, but this numbering is not necessarily printed on the motherboard or, if it is printed, it is obscured by chips or other resident obstacles. The description that follows is of jumpers on a recent Pentium MMX board. This is fairly typical of modern practice on Socket-7 boards, and most boards that you are likely to come across will provide for a similar list of jumpers. Pentium-II boards are often jumperless.

One jumper is used to control CMOS RAM, and its default position keeps the CMOS RAM clear. This will have to be reset to the working position before the motherboard is installed. Another jumper sets the voltage supply for DIMM memory, usually to 3.3 V, with the alternative of 5 V.

A very important set of jumpers deals with CPU type and voltage. One jumper setting is for Pentium type, either P54C (dual voltage) or P55C (single voltage) types. Another set of jumpers will set the CPU (core) voltage to the required voltage in the set 2.5 V, 2.8 V, 2.9 V, 3.2 V, 3.3 V or 3.5 V. You need to set the jumpers for the exact voltage that your CPU chip needs.

That's easier said than done. Motherboard manuals are not always up to date, and a chip is often supplied with no data. A good rule is that the faster chips use lower voltages, so that if you replace a 166MMX used at 2.8 V with a 233MMX whose recommended voltage is 3.2 V you should be suspicious. The sure sign of using too high a voltage is that Windows and even some DOS commands (like DIR) will not run correctly. If reducing the core voltage restores normal operation, you can be certain that the higher voltage setting is incorrect, whatever the documentation states.

The next important settings are the internal clock speed jumpers which are set for the type of processor you are using. The settings are usually graded as 1.5×/3.5×, 2.0×, 2.5× and 3.0×, and the usual default is 2.0×. You will need to check the manual for the motherboard and any leaflets that come with the processor to know how to set this. Several modern motherboards can make this setting automatically by sensing the type of CPU that is inserted, and some jumper settings work differently with different processors. The other clock setting is labelled *External clock* and typically allows for bus speeds of 60 MHz, 66 MHz, 75 MHz, and 83 MHz. The 66 MHz speed is the usual default, and you will, once again, need to check carefully to find if you need to use a different speed.

- Note that the motherboard design fixes the maximum speed of CPU that you can use. At the time of writing, very few motherboards using Socket-7 provided for CPU speeds above 233 MHz.
- Raising the *External clock* speed is one way of making a chip work faster than the maker has intended, but you must not experiment unless you are prepared to lose your CPU. Some users have reported that this *overclocking* can be done safely on some chips, but it's on your own head if you do so and burn out the CPU. You also have to be certain that other chips will accept the higher rate.

Take your time, enquire if necessary, and do not install the motherboard into the case until you are totally satisfied that the jumper settings are correct. A familiar problem is that the documentation may tell you that the setting you want is to jumper pins 1 and 2, but there is no pin numbering on the motherboard. If you come across this problem, you will often find that you can deduce pin numbers by looking at other settings which you are fairly sure have been correctly preset. You may find, for example, that pin 1 is the pin closest to the end of the motherboard that contains the expansion slots.

Once the jumper settings have been dealt with and double-checked, you can install the CPU, unless this has already been done by the supplier. Normally, if you buy a board and a CPU by mail order, the CPU will have been inserted and the jumpers set, except for the CMOS RAM jumper. If you buy the motherboard

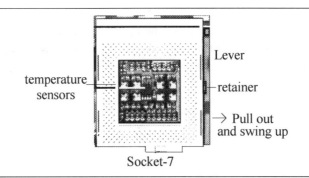

temperature sensors

Lever

retainer

→ Pull out and swing up

Socket-7

2.12 The lever at the side of a Socket-7 that is used to free or lock the pins of the CPU.

and processor separately (at a computer fair, for example), you will have to insert the CPU for yourself and also check that the jumper settings are correct.

Before inserting the CPU check that it is the type you ordered, and note which corner has a pin missing, a notch, and a white dot. Some fans come with a small tube of heat-sink grease (Electrolube) that helps in heat transfer, and you can order this separately from Maplin; it is no longer stocked by Tandy stores. Only a thin film is needed, and you should not have grease oozing out from between the fan and the chip. You can get away with omitting the grease on the slower chips such as the 166MMX type.

Pull the lever away from the body of the Socket-7 and then pull it upwards (Figure 2.12). A CPU for Socket-7 has a notched corner with a white dot to identify its pin 1 position, and this needs to be placed at the corner of the socket that has a hole missing and a figure 1 stamped on the socket. The CPU should drop into place, any resistance probably indicates that it is the wrong way round. You can then fit the cooling fan. This item clips over the top of the chip, and the clips are very strong because they have to keep the fan in very close contact with the chip. You will need to support the motherboard with your fingers to avoid excessive flexing when you press down the clips on the fan.

Following these settings of jumpers and CPU insertion you will need to install memory, and on all modern motherboards this is usually done using EDO SIMMs. Connections are made to the SIMM just as they are to expansion cards, using an edge connector, a set of tiny metal tongues on the card which engage in springs on the holder. Nowadays these EDO SIMMs come in sizes from 8 Mbyte per SIMM to 32 Mbyte per SIMM. Currently you should not put more than 64 Mbyte total into the motherboard (which usually takes 128 Mbyte or more) unless you are certain that your operating system will cope with a memory of more than 64 Mbyte.

This does not mean that you can expand a 16 Mbyte computer to 32 Mbyte by adding a 16 Mbyte SIMM. The usual arrangement is that SIMM units must be installed in twos, so that you can expand by 16 Mbyte at a time using the 8 Mbyte SIMMs and by 32 Mbyte at a time using the 16 Mbyte SIMMs. Check with the manual for your computer to find what arrangement is needed. This is particularly important if your motherboard provides for DIMM units as well as for EDO SIMM. The DIMM boards do not (currently) have to be inserted in pairs, but you may not be able to use DIMM along with SIMM.

Each EDO SIMM is installed by slotting it in at an angle of about 45° and then straightening it up, when two plastic clips hold it in place. DIMM units come in several types, and there are two notches in each DIMM board that must match with the socket to ensure that only the correct type of DIMM will fit. One notch determines voltage supply (3.3 V, 5.0 V or reserved); the other is marked *Unbuffered*, *Buffered* or *Reserved*. The reserved positions are likely to be used when new varieties of DIMM boards are manufactured.

Motherboard assembly

Once the CPU and memory units have been inserted, the motherboard can be mounted into the casing, but don't rush into this task. Very often when a Baby AT motherboard is in place, part of it lies under the power supply unit, and because of this the PSU is often supplied separately, not connected in. The ATX layout is much better in this respect. If you are working with a Baby AT board, don't connect in the PSU at this stage, and if the casing has come with its PSU fastened into place, check with the motherboard locating point to see if any of the motherboard will be covered by the PSU. If it is, as is normal, you must remove the PSU by unscrewing the three small bolts at the rear of the case and the three underneath.

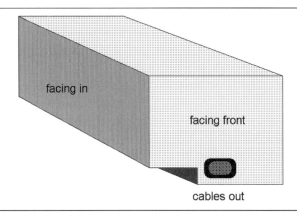

facing in

facing front

cables out

2.13 The shape of the usual Baby AT power supply box. The motherboard lies under the overhanging portion.

If your PSU uses a different number of bolts, make a note of this. A miniature socket set is useful for these bolts.

- It is particularly difficult to plug in the power connectors to the Baby AT board if the PSU is in place, and you may also have difficulties with the IDE connectors and the ports.

With the PSU laid temporarily out of the way, you can now concentrate on the motherboard mountings. Metal cases for the PC have their locating fasteners in standardized positions, and motherboards are provided with matching location holes, so that it is very unusual to find that there are any problems in fitting a new motherboard. Do not expect, however, that a new motherboard will have exactly as many mounting holes as there are fasteners on the casing, or that all of the mounting holes will be in the same places. Remember, though, that a motherboard should *never* be drilled because the connecting tracks on the surface are not necessarily the only tracks that exist; most boards are laminated with tracks between layers. Drilling through any of these tracks would be a very expensive mistake.

The fitting methods vary, but the most popular systems use either a brass pillar at each fixing position or a plastic clip at some positions. The brass connectors are screwed into threaded holes in a case and the motherboard is bolted in turn to the pillars; the plastic clips that fit into slots in the case are pushed into the holes in the

BUILD AND UPGRADE YOUR OWN PC

motherboard and then slotted in place. There should be at least one brass pillar fixing that is used to earth the motherboard electrically to the casing. Quite often, only two screwed fittings are used, with the rest being either clips or simply resting points. The motherboard must be well supported under the slots, because this is where pressure is exerted on it when cards are plugged in. If there are no supporting pillars in this region you may be able to get hold of polypropylene pillars of the correct size and glue them to the floor of the casing – do not under any circumstances glue anything to the motherboard itself.

- You may find that some plug-in actions, notably the CPU fan fitting, will bend the motherboard. Always support the motherboard by hand if it looks like flexing excessively. Flexing is one sure way of cracking motherboard tracks, and you would find it very hard to find the breaks or to make repairs. Worse still, you might find that the computer had intermittent faults due to a cracked track making intermittent disconnections.

When you have the motherboard in place, check everything again. It is remarkably easy to plug in jumpers with only one pin making contact, for example, and when you come to make other plug and socket connections this is also a hazard to look out for. If the paperwork that came with the motherboard did not have a sketch of the motherboard, this is the time to make one for yourself that shows where the board is mounted and where the jumpers are. Remember that it is often very difficult to alter jumpers once a motherboard has been fitted in place, particularly if the jumpers are underneath the power supply box.

- On a Baby AT board that contains connectors for power input and for disk drives, you should consider fitting the cable connectors at this point, because they can be very difficult to reach when the PSU box is in place. In addition, you can support the motherboard more easily with the PSU box out, and ensure that the plugs are correctly inserted. This does not absolve you from checking these plugs again afterwards, because in the course of connecting up these plugs can (and do) work loose, cause problems with hard drive and CD-ROM use.

You now need to reinstall the PSU box if you removed it earlier. If you are fitting a PSU that came separately packaged the first requirement is to check that you have all the mounting bolts – these are usually American UNF or M5 metric types which are not easy to replace, certainly not at your local ironmonger or DIY store. The second point is that the PSU has to be slid rather carefully into the casing, ensuring that the weight of the PSU does not rest on the motherboard. This is more difficult if the older design is used with a switch at the side. The thick and stiff set of cables from the PSU makes this task of fitting more difficult than you might expect. The shape of the PSU box allows part of the motherboard to lie underneath it without touching the components on the motherboard. Once the mains switch is located, it is easy to position the PSU so that all the screw holes line up, and the bolts can be put in place, finger-tight at first.

As you tighten the bolts, check that the mains switch, if it is on the PSU box, can be operated easily. Some casing slots are a tight fit for the switch, and if the PSU mountings are a fraction out of line the switch will jam or be stiff. This can usually be avoided by moving the PSU slightly on its mountings as you tighten the bolts, but you may need to file the slot to get a perfect fit. If this is needed, take the PSU out again, and file with the outside of the slot pointing down, avoiding any filings landing on the motherboard. Tap the casing afterwards to remove any lurking filings – just one filing bridging tracks can cause puzzling symptoms and no one can run a diagnostic test and instantly exclaim: 'Yes, of course, you have a steel filing bridging two tracks.' Most modern casings have a main switch that is on the end of a cable and which plugs into the front of the casing.

Before the PSU is bolted into place, using a Baby AT board, the two main plugs must be inserted into their sockets on the motherboard. These plugs are made so that they fit together in a line, and they should plug in one way round only. When you are replacing an old board, it is easy to mark the plugs so that you can see which way round they go, but with nothing to guide you it is considerably more difficult, particularly since the two plugs look almost identical, Figure 2.14. If there is nothing else to guide you, the way that the plugs are arranged on the power supply cable is usually a good clue – if you have to bend, twist or rearrange the cables you are almost certainly putting the plugs into the wrong positions. The

rear

front

2.14 The shape of the two Baby AT power plugs. These are retained in place by a plastic clip on each half.

plugs have to be inserted so that they are clipped into place, and this can take a considerable amount of effort. The 20-pin plug for an ATX board is easier to insert.

The connections for the two different types of connector are listed below.

Baby AT board

Pin	Use	Pin	Use
1	Power good	7	Earth
2	+5 V DC	8	Earth
3	+12 V DC	9	−5 V DC
4	−12 V DC	10	+5 V DC
5	Earth	11	+5 V DC
6	Earth	12	−5 V DC

ATX board

Pin	Use	Pin	Use
1	3.3 V DC	11	3.3 V DC
2	3.3 V DC	12	−12 V DC
3	Earth	13	Earth
4	+5 V DC	14	Power on
5	Earth	15	Earth
6	+5 V DC	16	Earth
7	Earth	17	Earth
8	Power OK	18	−5 V DC
9	5 VSB	19	+5 V DC
10	+12 V DC	20	+5 V DC

Note: The 5 VSB line is a standby supply which should be capable of operating with a 10 mA load.

Chapter 3

About disk drives

The use of a 3.5″ floppy drive is one of the few really noticeable external differences between the early PC type of machine and the PC/AT machines that started to appear at the end of the 1980s. The same system of recording and replaying heads is used for hard drives as for the floppy type, though the spacing between the disk surface and the heads is usually much smaller. In addition, the larger capacity hard disk units use multiple disks with two heads per disk. As Chapter 1 has pointed out, a PC must use both a hard drive and a floppy drive. This is a minimum, and there is nothing to stop you having more than one of each provided that you have suitable cables and driver cards. Hard drives for desktop machines are predominantly of the 3.5″ type, but the Quantum Bigfoot type uses the 5.5″ size, and hard drives for portable machines are a standard 2.5″ type. Floppy drives are of a standard pattern, though you may find some machines equipped with a high-capacity drive that will accept the standard floppy or a 100/120 Mbyte version.

The floppy drive

When you insert a 3.5″ floppy disk into a drive a hub spins briefly

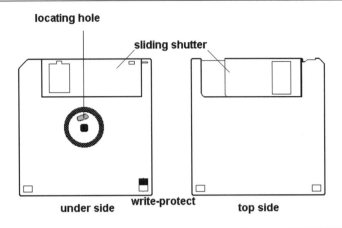

locating hole

sliding shutter

under side   write-protect   top side

3.1 The 3.5″ floppy disk in its plastic case. The additional hole opposite the write-protect aperture is recognized by the computer so that the disk will be formatted as 1.4 Mbyte.

until the key in the drive shaft engages the slot in the disk, Figure 3.1. The act of inserting the disk also draws aside the shutter which normally protects the disk surface from air-borne contamination. When the drive is used, the drive motor starts to spin the disk at a speed of about 300 revolutions per minute.

The disk itself, Figure 3.2, is a circular flat piece of thin plastic which has been coated with magnetic material on each side. Through the slot that is revealed when the shutter is drawn aside, the heads of the disk drive can touch the surface of the disk, one head on each side. These heads are tiny electromagnets, and each head is used both for writing data and for reading data. When a head writes data, electrical signals through the coils of wire in the head cause changes of magnetism. These in turn magnetize the disk surface. When the head is used for reading, the changing magnetism of the disk as it turns causes electrical signals to be generated in the coils of wire.

The heads of the disk drive move along a radial path. If the head is held steady, the spinning disk will allow a circular strip (sometimes incorrectly referred to as a 'cylinder', which ought to mean a collection of these strips on several disks) of the magnetic material to be affected by the head. By moving the head in and out, to and

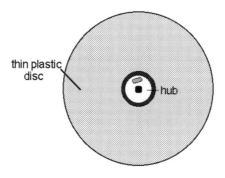

thin plastic disc

hub

3.2 The thin plastic disk inside the case is coated with magnetic material.

from the centre of the disk, the drive can make contact with different circular strips of the disk.

These strips are called 'tracks', Figure 3.3, and unlike the groove of a conventional record, these are circular, not spiral, and they are not grooves cut into the disk. The track is magnetic and invisible, just as the recording on a tape is invisible. What creates the tracks is the movement of the recording/replay head of the disk drive as the disk spins. The number of tracks that you use therefore depends on your disk drives. The standard modern PC floppy disk system uses 3.5″ disks with 80 tracks on each side. The tracks are packed to the tune of 135 per inch, so that 80 tracks occupy only about 0.6

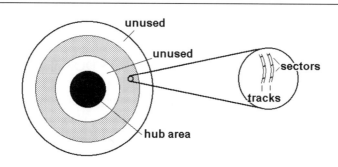

unused

unused

sectors

tracks

hub area

3.3 Tracks and sectors on a floppy disk. These are magnetized areas and are not visible.

inches of radius. These disks are known as high density, abbreviated to HD.

Once you have accepted the idea of invisible tracks, it's not quite so difficult to accept also that each track can also be invisibly divided up. The reason for this is organization – the data is divided into 'blocks', or sectors, each of 512 bytes. A byte is the unit of computer data; it's the amount of memory that is needed for storing one typed character, for example. Each track of the disk is divided into a number of 'sectors', and each of these sectors can store 512 bytes of data. The 3.5″ disk will record 18 sectors of data on each track.

Looking at the arithmetic of this, using two sides each of 80 tracks and 18 sectors of 512 bytes per track gives a grand total of $2 \times 80 \times 18 \times 512$ bytes of storage, which is 1 474 560 bytes. If we take 1024 bytes per kilobyte and 1024 kilobytes per megabyte this comes to 1.406 Mbyte. These disks are usually advertised as being 1.44 Mbyte, a figure that is obtained by imagining that 1 megabyte is 1000 Kbyte rather than 1024 Kbyte. This is at least smaller than the factor that is used to boost the prices of US books on computing.

A disk formerly called a *system disk* (now called a *startup* disk) is one that can be used at the time when the computer is first switched on (booted). This allows you to start your computer running before the hard drive is formatted, though you can use only MS-DOS when the machine is started in this way. A floppy system disk contains the MS-DOS tracks, 13 tracks that are reserved for holding the hidden DOS files, leaving 67 tracks for your use. You would normally keep these MS-DOS tracks on the hard drive, however, so that on all but a few of your 3.5″ floppy disks only 33 sectors are reserved for the main 'directory' entries, leaving the rest free. This corresponds to a total of 1 457 664 bytes free on such a disk if you format a disk without copying over the MS-DOS files. This type of disk is a data-only disk. You would normally use such disks to contain backup data such as wordprocessor text, data from spreadsheets or database or other programs, and short programs which you might use along with others rather than in their own right. You would keep a couple of disks also which contain the MS-DOS hidden files and a few other files such as CONFIG.SYS and AUTOEXEC.BAT (see later) to use as backup system disks in the event of problems with the hard drive. A system disk should also contain the MSCDEX.EXE file that enables the CD-ROM drive to be used if you cannot boot from the hard drive. Any system or start-up disk made using Windows 98 will contain a CD-ROM driver so that you can install Windows from CD-ROM even if the hard drive is not available.

The next thing that we have to consider is how the sectors are marked out. Once again, this is not a visible marking, but a magnetic one. The system is called 'soft-sectoring'. The 3.5″ disk has a shaped drive plate on one side, as illustrated in Figure 3.1 earlier. The drive hub has a pair of shaped pins that engage in the slots of the driveplate, and the first sector position is at a fixed point relative to the drive shaft. The software action called *formatting* will then place magnetic markings on the disk, taking this first sector point as a starting position.

When you load a program from a disk, or save data on a disk, you don't have to worry about the tracks and sectors. You don't, for example, have to specify at which sector and on which track the recording must start, and what to do if there is already something recorded on some of the sectors. All of this is the main action of the Disk Operating System (DOS), a sort of good-housekeeping system for disks, in conjunction with the disk controller circuits. The action of the DOS is to ensure that a disk is of the correct format, to keep a record of what sectors are used for what files, and to allocate sectors as needed when data is recorded. See later for details of the File Allocation Table (FAT) for hard drives.

The 1.4 Mbyte floppy is, by modern standards, woefully inadequate for the distribution of programs, and it has been superseded on all modern machines by the CD-ROM. Though the conventional floppy is still a reasonable way of making small backups and for distributing some types of material such as text files, it is not ideal for larger documents such as DTP pages or camera-ready copy in Word format. Currently, there are several options for fitting larger capacity drives, and we shall look at tape backup systems later.

Another option is the high-capacity floppy system, storing 100–120 Mbyte on each floppy (using a special floppy). Windows 98 provides for the use of these high-capacity floppy drives, and the most useful versions can use the conventional floppy and the high-capacity floppy interchangeably. The trouble with this is that the capacity is not really high enough for some purposes, and the cost of a blank disk compares poorly with storage costs using other methods. Ultimately it looks as if the use of read/write CD drives will replace floppies.

- The most cost-effective method of making large backups (several Gbyte) is by using tape. Several types of tape drives can be obtained for internal fitting, and another option for the home user is to use an adapter that allows the backup to be made by a conventional video recorder (because videotape is so cheap compared to digital tape).

Hard drives

The floppy type of disk has several limitations. The main limitation is that the disk spends most of its life out of the drive, subject to the dust and smoke in the room where the disk is housed. The recording and replaying heads are in contact with the disk surface, so that the fragile floppy disk cannot be spun at a very high speed because of the friction of the heads and of the sleeve which protects it.

The hard drive, originally called a Winchester disk, is a way of obtaining a much larger amount of information packed into the normal size of a disk. The older name of Winchester was used because this was the IBM name for a project that called for the development of a hard disk in a sealed unit in the early 1970's. Like other types of hard disks, Winchesters keep the disks themselves and the magnetic read/write heads sealed inside a container that ensures a dust-free environment for the disks. Unlike some other types of hard drive units, however, the Winchester is permanently sealed the disks (more correctly, *platters*) are not removable, and the sealing will be disturbed only if repairs are needed, and that will require an air-conditioned workshop. This sealing into a clean dust-free space allows the gap between each head and its disk to be made much smaller than could be contemplated for a floppy disk, smaller than a grain of dust or a particle of smoke.

- Removable hard drive units that are used for backup drives keep the disk platters in a sealed cartridge.

The same system of using recording and replaying heads is used

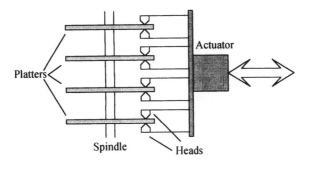

3.4 How hard drive platters and heads are arranged.

for hard disks as for the floppy type, though the heads are never in contact with the disk surface; they float on a thin film of air. In addition, hard disk units use multiple disks, made of coated aluminium, with two heads per disk, using anything from two to 17 disks (or platters) in a drive. The very small gap between the head and the platter allows a much higher packing of information on to the platter so that the most obvious effect of using a hard drive is the much greater number of bytes that can be stored. Figure 3.4 shows a typical arrangement of platters and heads. All of the heads are moved in step, so that at any particular time each head will be positioned over the same track on each side of each platter, and this set of tracks is called a *cylinder*.

Unlike the comparatively slow-spinning floppy disk, the hard drive spins at a very high speed, around 3600 revolutions per minute for the older types to 7 200 rpm or more in recent models. This means that the rate at which data can be written to the drive or read from it is much greater, at least 12 times as fast as a floppy disk. This speed of recording or recovery of data has been helped by the progress in reducing the size of these hard drives. The first units used 14″ drives, and by the late 1970s 8″ units were in full production. The modern 5.25″ hard drive started to appear by the early 1980s, and the 3.5″ size in the mid-1980s, but it is only recently that prices have dropped to a level that allows really widespread use of hard drives on small computers. Recently, the 5.25″ size has reappeared as a low-cost high-capacity drive.

Recording methods

Basically, the writing action of the disk head consists of magnetizing the surface of the spinning disk with a set of signals that correspond to the data that is being recorded. Reading the disk is done by the reverse action, allowing the varying magnetization of the disk track to affect the coil of wire in the reading head, providing the electrical signals. There are, however, many possible ways of coding electrical signals into magnetization of a disk track, and you will find references in older books to systems called FM and MFM. As far as the IBM PC type of computer is concerned, the system that is used is not important, because the EIDE (or ATA) type of hard drive contains the electronic circuits that carry out the coding and decoding, and no separate card or motherboard circuits are needed.

- All hard drives now use a voice-coil type of mechanism which is similar in principle to the mechanism of a loudspeaker. This allows track spacing to be set by electronic rather than mechanical methods, so that software can be used to change the number of tracks and their spacing. It also ensures that the head is not over important tracks when the drive is idle, so that you are much less likely to damage the drive if the computer is knocked while the power is off.

Simply having a disk drive in place is not sufficient, however, because hardware and software are needed to make the disk operate. On the old PC machines, the disk driving hardware was on a plug-in card separate from the disk drives. On modern machines, the driving circuits for the hard drive are on the drive itself – hence the name of Integrated Drive Electronics (IDE) for this type of drive. Computers using this type of hard drive, more than 90% of all PC machines, have an IDE (or *ATA*) interface which usually includes floppy disk drivers for up to four floppy drives, along with interfacing for up to two hard drives and ports for printer and serial connectors. This is usually located on the motherboard, and is nowadays the extended (EIDE) type, with both a primary and a secondary drive connector, each capable of driving two devices. The conventional way of using this is to have a hard drive on the primary connector and a CD-ROM drive on the secondary connector. A second hard drive can be connected to the cable of the primary connector.

- Larger computers that are used for file servers use the older but very capable SCSI (Small Computer Systems Interconnection) systems that allow one driver card to serve a large number of drives. SCSI connectors are also used for a variety of other devices such as scanners, and should be used if you need a large number of drives and other devices that interchange data at a high speed. You need some knowledge of SCSI methods if you are to make use of this system, and a deeper pocket to pay for the SCSI interface card.

Using EIDE/ATA, there is a 40-strand data cable which connects from the IDE board primary IDE connector to the hard drive (or to each of two hard drives). A separate cable from the power supply unit is used to provide power for the motors of both the hard and floppy drives. The secondary EIDE connector is used with a similar cable to connect to the data socket of the CD-ROM drive.

FAT16 and FAT32

One important factor about hard drives is that the manufacturing techniques have run ahead of the development of operating systems, so that very large-capacity hard drives can now be sold at low prices. When MS-DOS was adapted for hard drives, a 16-bit binary number was allocated for storing the number of memory units on the disk. This stored number is used in a File Allocation Table (FAT) that allocates a number for each unit of data, and the electronics of the hard drive can convert each FAT number into a location on the hard drive in terms of track and sector numbers. A 16-bit binary number can store up to 65 536 units, and if each is a 512 byte sector, that limits total storage to 65 536/2 Kbyte (because 512 bytes is 0.5 Kbyte). This would limit disk storage size to 32 768 Kbyte, or 32 Mbyte, and this was about the maximum size of the first hard drives.

In the early days, this seemed quite adequate, but as programs grew in size and generated large amounts of data, the limit became a problem that was solved by using *clusters*. A cluster is a set of sectors, and if we use clusters of 8 sectors (4 Kbyte) then our number 65 536 corresponds to $65\,536 \times 4 = 262\,140$ Kbyte, about

255 Mbyte. This extended the use of hard drives, and the solution was to use a different number of clusters for each size range of hard drive. For example, using 32 Kbyte clusters permitted the use of a hard drive of 2048 Mbyte, 2 Gbyte in size. This could be doubled by using 64 Kbyte clusters.

All of this, however, leads to inefficiency. Suppose you need to store ten small items of data, each 128 bytes (such as shortcuts to Windows programs). Each of these has to be stored on a cluster of its own, because otherwise there is no way of finding it on the disk – each item must correspond to a number in the FAT. This made the use of large hard drives inefficient, and one solution in the past was to partition the drive, divide it up before formatting it into a set of drive letters as if there were a set of separate small drives, each with a smaller cluster size. Another solution was the use of Microsoft's DriveSpace utility, which could pack each cluster with data and use another reference number to find the position of the data in the cluster.

In Windows 98, and on the later (1997 onwards) version of Windows 97, the FAT32 system has been used on all new machines. As the name suggests, this uses a 32-bit FAT, allowing the storage of numbers up to 4 294 960 000 and so greatly extending the size of disks that can use 4 Kbyte clusters. If you use Windows 98, you can convert a hard drive that has used the FAT16 system to use the FAT32 system, without the need to reformat the drive and lose the data. The (OEM) version of Windows 95 that used FAT32 was not made available to individual users, only to manufacturers, because it did not contain any utilities for preserving the data on a drive.

Fitting a hard drive

- When a new hard drive is fitted, it will have to be partitioned, formatted and then have programs, starting with Windows, installed. Do not assume that you can easily transfer Windows or other programs to a new formatted drive from an existing hard drive. The copying action is easy enough, but getting the programs to work is quite another because the copied programs will not take up the same positions on the new drive as they had on the old. This is no problem for many programs, but where there is interaction between programs (as with Windows and Word, for example) you will run into problems.

We need to look at the installation of a hard drive first, because it is normal to keep the hard drive in the lowest of the drive bays of a set, making it inaccessible once the floppy drives have been fitted. A built-in drive is the logical method of adding a hard drive to any machine which is of the standard PC type of construction, with a set of drive bays at the front of the casing. It is also the obvious system for slimline cases, provided that there is space, and for the tower type of unit if you can gain easy access.

The ordinary full-sized desktop case, particularly if it uses the conventional flip-top lid, is reasonably easy to work with, even if it does take up a lot of room on the desk (a bigger desk is usually cheaper than a smaller computer). A good design of midi-tower is also very easy to work with, but some smaller towers can be cramped for space. On some machines, you might have to remove some bays to get access to the bay that will be used for the hard drive.

Do not assume that a drive will be provided with mounting brackets at exactly the same places as the drivebay, though these positions are usually standard on PC clones. An adapter will be needed if you want to put a 3.5$''$ hard drive into a 5.25$''$ bay, but modern cases should be well provided with 3.5$''$ drive bays. You should enquire when you order or buy the drive what provisions are made for mounting it on the style of casing you are using. Make sure that all mounting bolts and connecting cables are supplied with the drive.

- Drive fittings are particularly important if you are upgrading an old machine because some manufacturers, notably Amstrad, used mounting systems which were very different from the IBM type of design, and even some IBM cases seem to use non-standard fittings.

The drive bay normally has slots at the sides to allow for to and fro adjustment of a drive, and two sets are usually provided at different heights in the bay. These should fit the hard drive in a 3.5$''$ bay without any problems and also fit a 5.25$''$ bay using an adapter plate. Hard drives must be mounted to the bay or the adapter plate by way of small bolts fitting into their threaded mounting

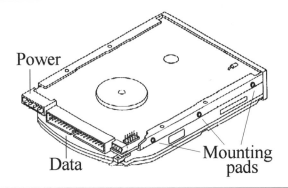

Power

Mounting
pads

Data

3.5 The mounting pads for a typical hard drive.

pads. This is important because these pads act to cushion the drive against shock.

- In no circumstances should you consider drilling the casing of a hard drive in order to mount it in any other way. You should also handle a hard drive by its casing, not holding its weight on any other points. In particular, avoid handling the connector strips at the rear of the drive or any of the exposed electronic circuits. Read any documents that come with the hard drive to find if there are any prohibitions on the use of mounting holes – sometimes you are instructed to use only the outer set of holes.

The 5.25″ type of hard drive, usually large capacity drives, will fit into any bay of this size with no need for adapters. The 3.5″ drives use underside mountings as well as side mountings, which make it easier to attach them if the side fastenings are difficult to reach. If you have problems, Meccano brackets and strips can usually ensure that you get the drive unit firmly fastened. In a desperate situation, there is nothing wrong with fastening the drive to a metal plate and sticking this to the casing with self-adhesive foam pads. Maplin supply very useful sideplates for fitting a 3.5″ drive into a 5.25″ bay.

Jumpers and switches

The simplest possible installation of a hard drive is as the first hard drive in a machine which has only one floppy drive; or the replacement of an existing hard drive with an identical type. Complications arise only when a second (or further) hard drive is being installed, or when there are uncertainties about the compatibility of parts. The methods that are required vary according to the type of drive that is being fitted, and in this book we shall concentrate on the EIDE/ATA type which is standard on modern PC machines.

An EIDE hard drive can be installed as a first (master) or a second (slave) drive. In normal circumstances, these will correspond to drive letter C and D respectively. The complication here is that these letters, known as logic drive letters, are assigned by the computer automatically, with both A and B reserved for use with the floppy drive(s), whether you have one or two floppy drives. The first hard disk will be assigned with the letter C, and other drives, such as CD-ROM, with letters D onwards.

Rather than talking about drive numbers or letters, though, it is preferable at this stage to talk about first and second hard drives. Some manuals will refer to these as hard drives 0 and 1, or 1 and 2. When you install a single EIDE drive on a machine, it should be configured as the *master* or only hard drive. This means that jumper settings have to be made to ensure that the hard disk signals are taken from the correct point in the computer, so that the operating system can make use of the disk. In technical terms, this is done by selecting the correct BIOS address number and the correct port address range on the controller board, see later. The settings are made by way of jumpers or DIP switches. For a first hard drive, these settings are almost always ready-made for you, and you need only check them. For a second hard drive, alterations will have to be made unless the suppliers have done them for you.

The main complication can arise if you are fitting a second hard drive in a machine which has used a single hard drive. You will need to alter jumper settings so as to configure the second drive as a *slave* of a pair of drives. On *older* drives, you will also need to take out the first hard drive (if it is already fitted) and configure this as the *master* drive of two. You will also need a data cable that has two hard drive connectors and which is long enough to reach drives that may be some distance apart. The documentation accompanying an EIDE drive is often very sparse, no more than a sheet of paper. Using modern drives, you do not normally have to alter jumpers on the master drive, only on the slave.

If you are installing a second EIDE drive in an existing computer, try to use a drive from the same manufacturer as the first drive, and cables to match. This will help to avoid any problems of incompatibility. If this is not possible, ask the suppliers to check that the new drive you intend to fit will be compatible with the first type. This is normally not a problem with modern drive types, but some makes of drive are notoriously temperamental in this respect.

- Using modern drives, you have less to worry about, as long as the drive is set correctly as master or slave.
- If you want to use more than two hard drives you will have to use a SCSI interface, and buy SCSI hard drives and suitable connecting cables. The drives must use different SCSI access numbers.

Installation

Before you start, check the drive package to make sure you have all of the mounting bolts, any adapter that is needed, cables (if not already on the computer) and instructions. Check that you have the necessary tools – a Phillips screwdriver (possible a plain-head type) and a pair of tweezers are usually needed. The bolts are usually either 6-32 UNC $\times$ 0.31 (5/16$''$) or metric M4 $\times$ 0.7-6H, but some drives use M3 $\times$ 0.5. UK suppliers use millimetre sizing for the length so that the size will show 5 rather than 0.5 or 6 in place of 0.6. The frame of the drive may be stamped with M for metric or S for UNC. If you need spare UNC bolts you will need to contact a specialist supplier, but the M4 metric types can be bought from electronics suppliers such as the well-known Maplin or RS Components.

At this stage, check that any jumpers or switches are correctly set. Once the drive is in place these will be impossible to reach. Use tweezers to manipulate these devices. It is not always obvious from the accompanying instruction what settings are needed, and though drives are often set ready for use in a standard type of machine you cannot rely on this. Jumpers will quite certainly need to be set if you intend to use more than one hard drive.

Unpack the drive carefully and read any accompanying manual carefully, particularly to check any prohibitions on drive fastening or mounting positions. No drive should ever be mounted with its front panel facing down, but most drives can be placed flat, or on either side. Check that any adapter plate fits into the mounting bay on the casing, and that all bolts and cable adapters (see later) are provided. The hard drive is usually placed as the lowest in a set of drives on a desktop casing, and in a position nearest to the mother-board in a tower casing. Check also that the drive data cable will reach from the EIDE connector on the motherboard to the drive – you may need to put the IDE board in a different slot if the cable is short (as they often are).

Fasten the 3.5″ drive to its bay or adapter, using the small bolts that are provided to bolt into the mounting pads. Tighten these up evenly and not excessively. If an adapter is used, bolt this into its bay. Check that you can still place a floppy drive above the hard drive unit. This latter point is important, because floppy drives have an exposed flywheel on the underside, and the slightest contact against this flywheel will prevent the floppy drive motor from spin-ning. There should be no such problems if the 3.5″ floppy drive is being mounted sideways in a bay specially provided for this purpose, because such a bay is usually well clear of any others.

Installation is not a particularly skilled operation, though experi-ence with a Meccano set as a child is helpful. Problems arise only if the mounting pads on the drive do not correspond with openings in the bay, or you have no adapter for a 3.5″ or 2.5″ drive, or an unsui-table adapter, or you manage to lose a mounting bolt. A mounting bolt that falls inside the drive casing or the computer casing can usually be shaken out. Do not use a magnet to retrieve a bolt from a disk drive casing. Do not attempt to make use of other bolts, par-ticularly longer bolts or bolts which need a lot of effort to tighten (because they are ruining the threads in the drive). It is better to mount a drive with only three bolts rather than to add one bolt of the wrong type.

EIDE/ATA interface

Now connect up the cables to the drive(s). There are two sets of cables required for any hard drive, the power cable and the data cable set. The power cable is a simple four-strand type with a four-way connector (some drives use only two connections of the four).

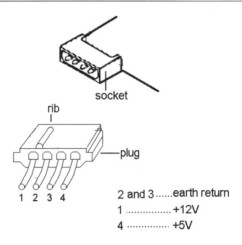

socket

rib

plug

1 2 3 4

2 and 3......earth return
1 ....+12V
4 ....+5V

3.6 Fitting the power cable connector.

This connector is made so that it can be plugged in only one way round. The same power cable is used for floppy drives and for hard drives, and modern AT machines usually provide four or five plugs on the cable. The plug is a tight fit into the socket and usually locks into place. The socket for the power plug is obvious, Figure 3.6, but some disk drives need an adapter which should be supplied.

The data cable that connects to the IDE drive is of the flat 40-strand type. This plugs into the matching connector on the motherboard at one end and into the drive at the other, with no complications. Look for one strand of the cable being marked, often with a black, striped or red, line, to indicate pin 1 connection. This makes it easier to locate the connector the correct way round. Do not assume that one particular way round (such as cable-entry down) will always be correct, or that a second hard drive will have its pin 1 position the same way round as your first hard drive. The power connection is as for any other system.

● The conventional system is to use the IDE plug at the end of the cable for the master drive and the other connector for a slave drive.

When you have the hard drive running satisfactorily, see later, it is desirable to mark the cable connectors so that you can replace them correctly in the event of having to remove the drives for servicing. Use Tippex or other white marker on the top side of each connector and write on the use (DATA1, DATA2, POWER1, POWER2 and so on). Mark also the pin 1 position on the cable and on the drive.

Checking out

When a hard disk, whatever the type, has been installed so that all the relevant steps described above have been carried out, you can check that the disk is mechanically capable of use. Check first that all connectors are firmly in place. It is quite common to find that all your efforts in plugging in the hard drive end of the cable have loosened the other end that plugs into the Primary EIDE socket on the motherboard.

You need to make the machine ready for use. Plug the keyboard connector into its socket on the motherboard – this is usually a DIN-type socket located at the back of the machine close to the PSU. Insert the video graphics card that you intend to use, easing the card into its slot and screwing it into place. Plug the monitor data cable into the socket on the graphics card. Insert the monitor mains plug – if this is a Euroconnector it can be plugged into the socket on the PC main case, otherwise use a standard mains plug for the moment.

With all cables plugged into their correct places and the lid shut, switch on the power. If the monitor is separately powered make sure that it is plugged in and switched on. You should hear the high-pitched whine of the hard disk drive motor start and settle to its final speed.

If you hear a lot of disk activity and the machine boots (possibly with some error messages) then the hard disk is already formatted, and the formatting steps noted in Chapter 6 can be ignored. Congratulate yourself – you have avoided several tricky steps. This is as far as you can go for an unformatted hard disk, because you cannot use the drive until it has been formatted, but IDE drives which have been pre-formatted can often be put into service with little additional effort. If this is a second drive you have added, you can check that the machine is still booting up correctly from the first drive, and that the second drive is recognized. You can, however, check that the new hard drive is recognized in the CMOS RAM settings, see later.

- Normally, a hard drive is supplied with no formatting, and you have to use both the FDISK utility and the Format command, see Chapter 6.
- Some hard drives feature SMART, meaning self-monitoring and reporting technology. If your new hard drive has this feature you might need to look for a CMOS-RAM entry to ensure that it can be used. Once SMART is installed, disk problems will be notified.

Problems, problems

At this stage, unless the machine has booted from the new drive, you do not really know whether you have any major problems, because all you can tell is whether the hard drive motor is running or not. If there is no sound from the drive, particularly when you are using a single hard drive, then the drive motor is not running. Check the power cable if the drive has just been installed or replaced. This requires you to switch off, disconnect the mains lead, remove the monitor and open the lid.

It is most unusual to have this problem, because the power supply cable can be inserted only one way round. It is possible, however, that if an adapter has been used it is incorrectly wired or that a wire is broken. Check also for any signs of a break in the power cable, particularly at the connector.

Another possible cause of a hard disk not starting is a head jamming slightly against a platter. This should *never* occur on a new drive, particularly on any modern type with self-parking heads, but if you have bought or transferred an old (to the point of being ancient) unit the problem can sometimes arise. The motor unit of a hard disk has a very low power output, particularly when it starts, so that only the slightest amount of friction is needed to make it stick. Even the metal strap over the drive shaft, which is used to prevent electrostatic charging, can exert enough force to make a motor reluctant to start.

The remedy, which sounds drastic and must never be used on a new drive, is to switch off, tap the hard drive gently and switch on, tapping again just at the instant of switch-on. This symptom can be a sign that the unit is failing, but very often the life can be extended very considerably by simply parking the disk heads. Units as old as this will use a stepper motor drive, so that the heads are not parked automatically each time the machine is to be switched off. You may never have the problem again if you use head-parking software. Note that this applies to really old drives, and all modern drives are self-parking.

Fitting the floppy drive

So much of the installation of a floppy drive follows the same pattern as fitting a hard drive that very little needs to be said here. Fitting a 3.5″ drive into a 5.25″ bay is done by way of an adapter kit, but this is most unlikely to be needed if you are using a modern casing. As before, take great care never to lose the fixing screws for these conversion holders and for drive bays, because they are types that are not easy to replace unless you have access to a computer shop with a good selection of hardware. Never assume that because a bay is provided this means that the cables supplied with the machine will be able to reach a drive added to that bay. Cables are often supplied that are so short as to restrict your layout seriously, and you may have to alter the positions of drives in the bays so that the drive with the shortest cable is closest to the motherboard.

Check in particular that there is clearance between the underside of the floppy drive and the drive beneath it. This is not a problem when the floppy drive is fixed on its side in a bay intended for this purpose, but when you need to fit a hard drive and a floppy drive into adjacent bays you may encounter problems. The problem, as noted earlier, is that the flywheel of a floppy drive is on its underside and can easily be fouled by any slight projection from the drive above it. The amount of leeway in the mountings usually allows you to separate the drives enough to avoid the problem.

That apart, the main points to note are that the floppy drive has its jumpers set for use as Drive A or 0, and that the power cable is correctly used. Power cables nowadays are fitted with two types of plug, one of the standard size for hard drives and a smaller type for some makes of 3.5″ drives. The plugs are easy enough to insert, but

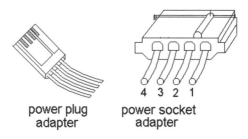

power plug
adapter

power socket
adapter

4 3 2 1

3.7 The power cable adapter that is needed for some makes of 3.5″ drive

it is not always easy to ensure that they are inserted correctly with all pins engaged. It is remarkably easy to insert a power plug with each of its pins against a piece of insulation rather than against the metal of a socket.

On the older versions of power units, all the power plugs are of the larger type, and an adapter, Figure 3.7, is needed to fit to some makes of 3.5″ units. This is straightforward, but if you do not have the adapter then you cannot proceed until you lay your hands on one. A good computer shop will often have some in stock. Remember to ensure that the connector to the 3.5″ drive is correctly inserted. The data connector should be plugged in the right way round, using the pin 1 marking on the data cable as a guide. Do not assume that the plug goes in with the cable facing down – this can vary from one cable to another. Inserting the data plug the wrong way round has not caused any damage when I have tried it, but the disk system does not work.

Testing a floppy drive is easy enough. With the machine set up with monitor and keyboard (see above), place an **MS-DOS** boot (see Chapter 8) disk into the drive that is to be the A drive (usually a 3.5″ type). Switch on, and wait to see evidence of activity from the drive. The machine should boot up if all is well.

If you are assembling from scratch, you should have a floppy that has been formatted as a system disk, with the **MS-DOS** tracks. This is essential if the hard drive is not formatted, because it allows you to format the hard drive and transfer the system tracks to the hard drive, allowing you to boot from then on directly from the hard drive. When you install Windows (see later) you should always take the option of creating a new system disk.

Chapter 4

Monitors, standards and graphics cards

Monitors

On the standard desktop type of computer, the image is produced on a *video monitor*, a phrase borrowed from television to mean a box which will produce a TV-style display on a screen of, typically, 33 cm diagonal or more. The details of monitors will be dealt with later in this chapter, but it is important to realize that a given monitor cannot be used with *any* type of computer graphics board because the types of signals have to be compatible. In particular, a monitor which will work with your video recorder will not necessarily be suitable for use with your computer, nor can you use a TV receiver with monitor signals unless a suitable interface card is present.

When you look at a TV display, you see a picture which is an illusion that is caused by the way that the human eye works. Though animals can sometimes respond to TV pictures, it is almost certain that they do not see the images that we see and are responding only to an impression of moving lights. All that actually appears on the screen is a dot of light which moves across and down the screen, varying in brightness as it goes. This movement is called *scanning*, and by making the dot return rapidly to its starting side of the screen

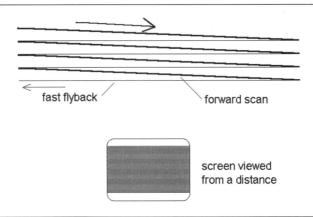

4.1 Principles of scanning, using a dot of light to create the illusion of an image.

after each scan across or down, the form of the scan is a single line. By making the horizontal speed of scanning much greater than the vertical speed, the form of the scan is a set of almost-horizontal lines that extend down the screen, Figure 4.1. This is the type of screen display that was envisaged by the true inventor of TV as we know it, Campbell Swinton, whose description is dated 1907. Altering the brightness of the spot as it scans will produce a picture in our eyes, because the action of the eye is chemical. The chemical change that is caused by light hitting the eye lasts for some 100 milliseconds, and anything that repeats faster than this appears uninterrupted or, at worst, with a noticeable flicker. TV pictures change at a rate of 25 per second (in the UK), and computer displays at, typically, 85 per second.

The *resolution* of a TV type of display means the amount of fine detail that can be displayed, and for TV purposes resolution is often quoted in terms of the number of vertical lines per screen width that can be clearly seen. Most domestic TV receivers are rather poor in this respect, even when new and well adjusted, and a resolution of only 300 lines is normal. This restriction is caused by the transmission system rather than by the ability of the cathode-ray tube to display the images, though in earlier days the tube was as much of a limitation. As always, a good monochrome system can usually permit better resolution, but the addition of colour is such a bonus to TV pictures that the loss of resolution is tolerable.

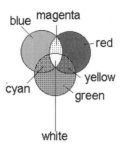

4.2 Using three primary colours to create a range of colours by mixing. Only a few mixtures are illustrated here, and all colours visible to the eye can be created by mixing the primaries in different proportions.

A monitor of professional quality used in a TV studio can produce pictures of quite staggeringly improved resolution, because such monitors can be connected directly to the TV cameras. The monitors that are used with computers are more closely allied to TV studio monitors (with some exceptions as we shall see later), and the resolution is also quoted in terms of dots per screen width, meaning the most closely spaced dots that can be distinguished on the screen. This is decided by the cathode-ray tube and the electronics circuits that control it, and it requires the dot of light that makes up all of the images to be very small. Some makers of monitors quote the average dot size in millimetres, but this is only useful as a way of comparing monitors of the same size. For example, a dot size of 0.50 mm is undoubtedly good on a 16″ monitor, but it would look rather less impressive on a 5″ monitor. The number of dots (called *pixels*, meaning picture elements) per screen width is a much better guide.

The reason that a mono monitor can always look clearer is that its dot is a single white dot, whereas colour monitors need to use three dots, one of each of the primary colours of red, green and blue, Figure 4.2. These are the primary colours of *light* incidentally – the primary colours of paint are the colours that the paint reflects. No matter how well a colour monitor is constructed it must make use of three dots (in practice, short stripes) to represent each point in an image, making its resolution inevitably lower than a monochrome monitor that is constructed to the same standards. This is why good-quality colour monitors are so expensive in the larger sizes, some £800 or more, in comparison to the £100 or so that will buy a monochrome monitor of excellent performance (if you could find one for sale in a size that is suitable). A few makers of monitors quote the dot pitch, meaning the distance between the colour dots in a set. This is not particularly useful unless you can translate it into final dot size; for example, a 0.31 mm pitch corresponds roughly to a 0.58 mm final dot size. Another complication is that the dot size on a monitor is not constant, it varies with intensity (bright dots are larger than dim ones) and with the position on the screen (the dot size is greater at the edge than in the centre). In general, a dot pitch of more than 0.32 mm on a 14″ screen is suited to resolutions of 640 × 480 or less and you need a pitch of 0.28 or less for resolutions up to 1024 × 768 on a 14″ screen. Note that monitors define screen size in the same way as TV receivers, measured along the screen diagonal. A 15″ screen of the modern flat section will look noticeably larger than one of the older curved shape, and the trend now is to monitor screens of 17″ or larger.

The CRT

The conventional cathode-ray tube (CRT) is cheap, but bulky, heavy, and power consuming. Readers with an electronics background will be familiar with the principles, but not necessarily in detail if they have specialized in topics other than television. If your previous experience has been in computing rather than in electronics, or if you have little experience of either, the following description may be helpful. If you are familiar with the topics, you can skip this section.

The principles of the mono cathode-ray tube (CRT) are shown in Figure 4.3. The screen is coated with a phosphor, meaning a material that glows when it is struck by particles such as electrons or by radiation like ultraviolet. There is no phosphorus involved; both names come from the same (Latin) root meaning *glowing in the dark*.

At the other end of the tube, the cathode that gives the tube its name, the tiny particles called electrons are torn away from atoms by a high temperature. They are then accelerated towards the

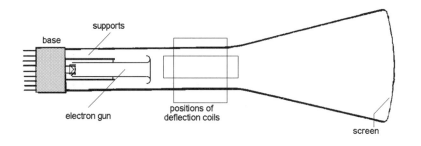

4.3 Diagram of a simple monochrome cathode-ray tube.

screen by a high voltage, typically 14 000–22 000 V (to put this in perspective, the mains supply in the UK is 240 V). The stream of electrons is forced into a beam by the metal cylinders in the electron gun, and is focused so that the diameter of the beam is a minimum where it hits the screen, forming the dot of light that appears on the screen. The beam of electrons is moved across and down the screen by a set of coils that fit over the neck of the tube. By passing current through a coil, the coil becomes magnetized and this will shift the position of the electron beam. By continually changing the current through a deflection coil of this type, the beam will be forced to scan across the screen at a steady rate, and by suddenly returning the current to zero, the beam can be made to return rapidly. The use of two coils positioned at 90° allows scanning in both the horizontal and vertical directions.

A colour display needs a much more elaborate type of tube, based on the original shadow-mask type of tube that was first produced by Radio Corporation of America in 1951. The principle of the modern version is that three different phosphors are used and are applied as sets of thin separate stripes down the inner surface of the screen. When struck by electrons, one phosphor will glow blue, another red, the third green, and the phosphors are laid in this striped pattern with the three always in the same order and with uniform spacing – there is usually a thin dark band separating the stripes. Instead of one electron gun, the colour tube uses three, and all three beams are focused and moved together. Near the screen, however, the beams have to pass through a set of slits in a stainless steel plate called the aperture grille (or shadow-mask), and this mask is the

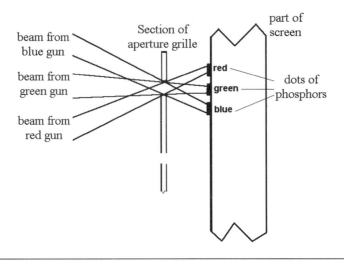

4.4 The arrangement of aperture grille and phosphor stripes that is used in a colour CRT.

point where the beams intersect. When a set of beams has passed through a slit in the aperture grille, the individual beams, which come from slightly different directions, will hit the phosphor stripe of the correct colour, Figure 4.4. The aperture grille prevents the beam from the red gun hitting the blue or green phosphors, and similarly prevents the beams from the blue and green guns hitting the wrong phosphor stripes. The size of the aperture grille stripes defines the pixel size for a colour tube.

The form of the colour tube means that a lot of the electrons on the beams are wasted because they land on the metal of the aperture grille rather than on the phosphor, and to make a colour tube look reasonably bright high voltage levels are needed to accelerate the electrons. Voltages of 14 000 to 22 000 V are used, and at the higher voltages the amount of X-ray generation in the tube starts to become measurable (meaning that it is almost as much as reaches us naturally from the Sun and stars). The use of lead glass for the tube reduces the penetration of such X-rays to a negligible amount, less than we receive from natural sources. The large colour tubes used for TV receivers use even higher voltage levels, with considerably more X-ray generation.

BUILD AND UPGRADE YOUR OWN PC

Dots and signals

The resolution of a monitor in terms of dots per screen width is just the start of the specification of a monitor for a PC. Nowadays, few users would want to make use of a monitor with fewer than 640 dots per screen width resolution, but the number of dots per screen width is not a complete guide to the suitability of a monitor. There is an additional factor, which is the way in which these dots are controlled.

The simplest way of controlling the dot brightness on a monitor is simply to turn the dot on or off, so that on means bright and off means dark. This scheme was used in the past for many mono monitors that are intended for mono display boards and is sometimes described as digital or TTL. The letters TTL refer to a family of silicon chips that make use of two levels of voltage, 0 and 5 V, for their input and output signals.

- If you see a modern monitor described as *digital*, it does not mean that this method is used, only that the signals are processed by digital circuits.

TTL signals are well suited to text, and can be used for a range of graphics shapes as well so long as you do not aspire to delicately shaded pictures. The first colour displays used these TTL signals applied to each of the colour primary signals, allowing a limited range of colours to be produced by using single colours or mixtures. Signals that use the three colour primaries in this way can produce red, green and blue using the dots for primary colours. They can also show the mixture of red and green, which is yellow, the mixture of red and blue which is magenta and the mixture of blue and green which is called cyan. The mixture of all three colours is white. Using a simple on–off scheme like this can therefore produce eight colours (counting black and white as colours).

The simple on–off method can be improved by using a fourth on–off signal, called brightness or luminance, whose effect when switched on is to make the colours brighter when this signal is switched on. This allows you to have black and grey, red and bright red, and so on, a range of 16 colours including black. This 16-colour system has been so common in the past that a lot of software still features 16 colours despite using a graphics system that allows a much greater range of colours. The 16-colour system is also called a 4-bit system, because four binary digits can be used to express each colour.

The alternative to digital signals is to use the *analogue* type of signal that is used for TV monitors, in which each signal for a colour can take any of a range of sizes or amplitudes. This method allows you to create any colour, natural or unnatural, by controlling the brightness of each of the primary colours individually. A monitor like this is much closer to TV monitors in design, and some (but certainly not all) monitors of this type can be used to display TV pictures from sources such as TV camcorders and video recorders. In this type of system, the signals from the computer are still digital, but each is converted to a different set of voltage levels before being applied to the tube. It's not just a matter of switching a colour on or off, but deciding how bright each colour shall be at each point on the tube face.

There are two varieties of analogue monitors, but the VGA type of monitor uses what is called the RGB set of signals. There is a separate connection for the three colour signals and for the other (synchronizing) signals as well, making the connector require more pins than would be needed for the other type, the composite signal type.

The alternative is a mixed signal which combines the separate RGB components into a single signal, as is done for transmitted TV signals, and is the type of signal that a video recorder will deliver at its video output socket. This means a simpler connection, with only one pin used on the plug for video rather than three or four, but it requires the monitor to separate the signals again, and the resolution will suffer slightly because of this extra processing. On the other hand, such a monitor could double as a monitor for a video recorder or camcorder – but that depends on the scanning system that is used as well. Composite signal monitors are *not* used for the PC.

This leads to the third point about monitors. All monitors use the line scan system, but for computing purposes this does not have to be identical to the method that is used for TV. Television has always used a form of scanning called interlacing, Figure 4.5, in which the odd-numbered lines (1, 3, 5, 7, etc.) are scanned, leaving a gap between the lines, for one screenful or *field*, and the even-numbered lines are then scanned, filling in the gaps, on a second field. Two such fields make up a complete picture frame.

This system was adopted when the TV system as we know it was

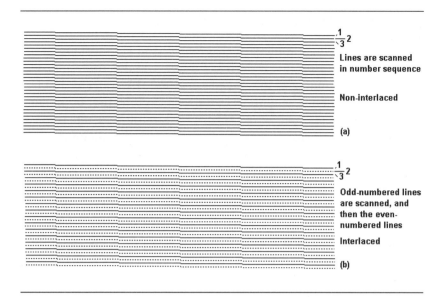

1
3 2

Lines are scanned
in number sequence

Non-interlaced

(a)

1
3 2

Odd-numbered lines
are scanned, and
then the even-
numbered lines

Interlaced

(b)

4.5   Interlacing, used for TV pictures but not on modern monitors.

first being designed in detail around 1935, and the reason was that it made the TV signals easier to transmit with the technology that was available at the time. The original rates of scanning that were chosen for TV allowed for the use of 405 lines at 50 fields per second in the UK, 525 lines at 60 fields per second in the USA. The UK and the rest of Europe then changed over to a scanning system of 625 lines and 50 fields in the mid-1960s, along with the colour TV system called PAL. The PAL system was adopted by most of Western Europe, apart (as usual) from France which used its own SECAM colour system and for some time used an 819-line scanning system. The American continent along with Japan stuck with the 525-line standard, now some 46 years old and beginning to look its age. US receivers also use the 1952-vintage NTSC colour system, and these differences in scanning rates and colour systems explain why you can't exchange video cassettes with friends in other countries.

For computing purposes, there is no need to be tied to TV scan rates, or interlacing, and the different TV colour systems refer only to the way that colour signals are transmitted, not to closed systems using monitors. In the UK, the 625-line TV picture is achieved by using a horizontal scanning signal that repeats at about 15 000 times per second. This is described as a 15 kHz scan, with k meaning kilo (one thousand when applied to electronics) and Hz meaning hertz, the unit of repetition rate in terms of number of repetitions per second. Some computer video systems use the TV rate of 15 kHz, others achieve better resolution in the vertical direction by making use of higher rates such as 22 kHz. The rate of field repetition is usually 60 or more rather than the European 50, though most monitors allow for adjustment to either rate. The important point is that your monitor must be suited to the computer – the computer graphics card decides on the scan rate and the monitor must be capable of using this rate. If your graphics card is an old one that uses a 15 kHz scan rate then buying an expensive monitor which can use a 22 kHz or higher scan rate will not improve the resolution. Either the monitor will not work, or it will work only at the scan rate of graphics board in the computer.

There is also a third requirement. The video signals are used to alter the intensity and/or colour of the dot of light as it moves across the screen, and the dot has to be in the correct place on the screen for each part of the signal. This requires the signals to be synchronized to the scanning, so that the first dot signals for a line arrive just as the scanning of the line has started. If this synchronization is not perfect then the picture will, at best, be misshapen, and at worst completely broken up and unrecognizable.

Synchronization is done by another set of signals, the *sync* signals, which are used to force the monitor to start a scan. There are two sync signals, one for each scan, with the line sync signals arriving at the line scan rate (15 kHz, 22 kHz or whatever standard is being used) and the field sync signals arriving at the field rate, usually 60 Hz or more. These signals can be taken along another two wires in the video cable to two more pins on the plug, or they can be combined with the video signals to make a composite video signal as used in television. Computer monitors for a PC machine work with separate colour and sync signals, but monitors for other computer types use a variety of methods, some using combined colour and sync signals inputs.

The unfortunate point is that computer manufacturers, unlike TV manufacturers, have no agreed standards. Some computers send out positive sync pulses, meaning that the voltage on the pin suddenly rises and very rapidly falls back to zero. Others use negative pulses, with the normally high voltage suddenly reducing and then returning almost immediately to normal. Some may even use positive pulses for one sync and negative for the other. Unless the monitor can be switched, preferably automatically, to recognize the correct pulse direction (or polarity), synchronization will be impossible.

This lack of standardization has led to the design of monitors which can cope with different scan rates and sync pulse polarities. These monitors are called *multisync*, using a name originally devised by the NEC Corporation when they made the first monitor of this type. Modern multisync monitors will adapt, usually automatically, to the scan rate and sync pulse polarity which they detect at the input, and will display a picture from most types of computer signals. This applies mainly to PC machines, however, and some of the mainly games machines which are still around demand very specialized monitors. Since these machine are unlikely to be used for serious purposes (other than DTP work), we can leave them out of consideration here.

Another point which causes a lot of confusion is the description of monitors as interlaced or non-interlaced. Whether or not a picture uses interlacing is determined by the synchronizing pulses that are sent out from the computer, not by the monitor itself. A monitor that is described as *non-interlaced* means one which will accept the high-resolution non-interlaced signals that are sent from graphics cards that use resolutions greater than 800×600. Higher resolution signals in turn demand that the monitor circuits can handle a much larger range of frequencies (the bandwidth), with bandwidths of more than 65 MHz being typical. As a comparison, the bandwidth of a good colour TV receiver is around 5.5 MHz. We should really refer to these monitors as wide-bandwidth rather than non-interlaced.

Video graphics cards

When the first IBM PC machine appeared in 1982, its provision for display was a simple black-and-white (monochrome) monitor of $12''$ diameter. Inside the computer, the numbers that are stored in the memory of the machine were turned into signals suitable for the monitor (video signals) by a separate circuit on a card that was inserted into one of the spare slots of the computer. The design of the machine allowed for adding on all kinds of extra facilities by way of cards which could be plugged into these expansion slots. Since the early machines provided almost nothing in the way of the facilities that we now take for granted (such as connecting printers, floppy disks, extra memory and so on) these slots were a very valuable way of upgrading the machine. Even today, when most PC machines come very fully equipped, a set of four to six vacant slots is still a very valuable part of the specification.

The original type of display was concerned only with text, because the concept of a machine for business use at that time was that only text, along with a limited range of additional symbols, was all that was needed for serious use as distinct from games. The video card was referred to as the Monochrome Display Adapter, a good summary of its intentions and uses, and usually abbreviated to MDA. It produced an excellent display of text, with each character built up on a 14×9 grid of the type illustrated in Figure 4.6. The text was of 80 characters per line and 25 lines per screen, and at a time when many small computers displayed only 40 characters per line using a 9×8 grid, this made text on the IBM monitor look notably crisp and clear. Typical monitors used a 18.4 kHz horizontal scan rate and 1000 lines resolution at the centre of the screen.

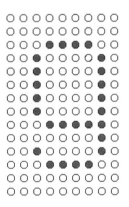

4.6 How a character is displayed on the old MDA type of display. A space must be left on each side if the characters are to appear separated.

     BUILD AND UPGRADE YOUR OWN PC

A monochrome monitor displaying text with the MDA video card still looks good, even by modern standards, but it is an obsolete component now. The only real fault, as far as text display was concerned, in the original IBM monitor display was that the monitor used a type of cathode-ray tube which is classed as high persistence. This means that the display faded out rather slowly, so that when one piece of text was replaced by another, the old version would fade slowly away rather than disappearing at once. This, however, makes the display very steady, with no trace of the flicker which many users find very disturbing, and most mono monitors, even now, are made with fairly long-persistence screens.

The other fault, however, was that graphics could not be displayed, so that graphs could not be produced from spreadsheets (on screen at least), and applications such as desktop publishing (DTP) or computer aided design (CAD) were out of the question. This latter point was purely academic at the time, however, because DTP did not exist at that time, and CAD was at an early stage of development on much larger machines. For a modern machine, however, no one would consider the MDA card or any other card that did not supply full modern graphics capabilities either in colour or in monochrome. That means a card of the type described as SVGA, and using a PCI (or AGP) local bus connection.

When IBM introduced their PS/2 machines in 1987, they broke to a considerable extent with the compatibility that had persisted from the early days of the PC machines and extended to the AT machines. The PS/2 machines no longer used a separate graphics card, a point of construction that was already being used by other manufacturers such as Amstrad. In addition, the PS/2 machines featured two new video display systems, MCGA (Multi-colour Graphics Array) and VGA (Video Graphics Array), and a new range of monitors which were analogue only. This meant that users of monochrome machines had to invest in new monitors, because up until that point monochrome machines had used Hercules-type cards with digital signals into the monitors.

The VGA card, however, has set the standard that business software has followed and is being widely emulated by other cards. VGA permits full compatibility with older systems. In addition it adds displays of 640×480 16-colour graphics and 800×600 colour graphics, using a 9×16 grid for characters with colour.

The VGA standard is so good that it has become a standard fitting, and no other graphics card is likely to be found on a modern machine. As a result dozens of suppliers have vied with each other to design and manufacture VGA cards. Some of the respected names in the video card business include ATI, Diamond, Genoa, Matrox, Orchid, Paradise and Video Seven, and many well-known brands of computers will be found to include graphics cards by one of these suppliers. In addition, there are many less well-known suppliers who use these cards or cards by equally less well-known manufacturers. As long as these cards are genuinely compatible with the IBM standard then there should be no problems with software.

The trouble comes mainly if you want to use 'enhanced features', making the VGA card into an SVGA card, with 'S' meaning super. You can find 640×480 resolution in 256 colours or even in 16 million colours, 800×600 in 16 or more colours and even 1048×768 or more in as many colours as you want. There is a trade-off between resolution and number of colours, because increasing either requires more memory for video, so that the amount built into the video card is often 2 Mbyte or even 4 Mbyte. Instead of quoting the number of colours in millions, it is more usual to quote the number of bits used to specify larger numbers of colours, such as 16, 24, 30, 32 or 36 bits. The number of colours is obtained by raising 2 to the power of the bit number, so that 16 bits give 2^{16} colours, which is 65 536 colours, and 36 bits gives 2^{36}, which is 68 719 400 000 colours.

If you are tempted to use higher resolution graphics it is important to remember that you will need a monitor that is capable of displaying the higher resolution. This will usually be a non-interlaced type of monitor. You will also need a graphics card with at least 2 Mbyte of memory, possible up to 4 Mbyte. Having done this, you may find the displays of words and icons so small that you need to work very close to the screen. This is undesirable, so that high resolution should be used only along with larger screens, and for purposes like image editing and DTP work for which it is desirable. This in turn makes it very expensive, and a very fast processor is needed to do justice to the system. The highest level of performance in terms of speed is needed if you want to show full-screen digital video pictures.

Choosing a graphics card

The PC is unusable unless a graphics card of some sort is fitted, and following the advice noted earlier you are likely to want to use an SVGA card of one variety or another. A quick flip through the computing magazines reveals that this is not a simple choice, because most suppliers can provide a considerable number of video cards at a huge range of prices, and monitors that follow similar patterns.

Here, as always, you need to think of what you need to use the computer for, and the trouble is that unless you have had some experience with a PC machine it is not easy to make an informed choice at this point. One item that can decide you is the general type of programs that you will use. Since it's likely that all or most of your programs will make use of the Windows system, then you need a graphics card that is fast working for Windows displays. If you intend to use resolutions higher than 640 × 480 you will need a video graphics card with at least 1 Mbyte of memory. You also need a card that will fit the PCI bus slots.

Another graphics card option is speed. The time needed to put a display on the screen can limit the speed of the PC machine when you are using Windows (see Chapter 9), so that several types of graphics cards have been developed which work faster at this task than others. Like Hi-Fi, you can pay a lot of money for fairly modest increases in speed, and for many purposes, the lower cost cards will suffice unless your interests run to full-screen video displays. The use of an AGP slot is now common on fast graphics cards.

- A lot of new machines are sold with graphics cards that offer much more than most users need or want, in the belief that we all use our computers for fast video, simulations of three-dimensional shapes, and instant displays of pictures from CD-ROM. If you are building your own you can concentrate on what you really want. If this is fast Windows use, then you can get a suitable card for a very reasonable price. If you are one of the few who uses the machine for video editing and video displays with 3-D effects, then you can go for one of the more costly graphics cards and a video card as well.

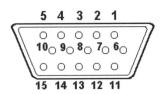

4.7 The shape of the standard VGA monitor data cable, as seen looking into the pins.

Connectors

The standard connector for VGA is a 15-pin D type, whose shape is shown in Figure 4.7. The pin use is as follows:

1	Red out	2	Green out
3	Blue out	4	NC
5	Earth	6	Red earth
7	Green earth	8	Blue earth
9	No pin	10	Sync earth
11	NC	12	NC
13	Horizontal sync	14	Vertical sync
15	NC		

Note: NC = No connection, pin not used. Pin 9 is removed to act as a key.

Drivers

For all normal purposes, your software will cope with a VGA card and its matching monitor without any intervention from you, provided that you are using standard text mode or 640 × 480 resolution graphics. When software is installed, you will be able to specify what video card and monitor (colour or mono) you are using, and by selecting VGA as the video card type, the system will automatically be configured to send out the correct signals.

Complications can arise if you want to use SVGA resolutions, typically 800 × 600 or higher. Contrary to what is sometimes suggested, you can run 800×600 even on a card with only 256 Kbyte of memory if you keep to a small range of colours. The main limiting factor is whether your monitor will permit the use of the different sync rates, typically 35.5 kHz and 57 Hz for horizontal and vertical respectively. Modern colour monitors are likely to be of the multi-sync type that will permit the change of frequency. The amount of memory in the SVGA board determines how many colours can be used in a picture.

What makes it rather less simple is the provision of drivers, meaning the software packages that adapt your programs to the resolution that the video card is using. Graphics cards generally come packaged with a disk that contains a set of these drivers, and some are of abysmal quality as well as being difficult to install. If you want to experiment with the higher resolution modes, and have suitable hardware, then the system outline here is a useful guide.

First of all, for the graphics card you intend to use, check to see if the Windows installation or setup program allows you to specify the use of 800×600 or whatever resolution you want to use for Windows. If this option appears, then the software can use the Windows driver, and this is likely to be better suited. If your graphics card is a type that is not recognized by Windows (which is unusual, because there are only a few basic designs) then you will have to use drivers for another card or drivers supplied on a floppy or CD along with the graphics card.

If you intend to use Windows for all your programs (including MS-DOS programs run from within Windows), the task is much easier because you need install only one high-resolution driver for Windows itself. You need to check that the Windows driver of your video card is suitable for the up-to-date Windows version. Before you install such a driver from the disk that comes with the video card, try some of the built-in Windows high-resolution drivers, as they are likely to be better. Use the setup program of Windows to install the driver, which usually involves inserting the Windows distribution CD to read files.

Chapter 5

Ports

Ports carry out the interfacing actions that are needed in order to connect a PC to other devices. Parallel ports are used to connect the computer to printers, and can also be used for other devices which need fast transfer of data, typically additional disk drives, scanners, and tape streamers. A parallel port deals with a byte of data (8 bits) in the transfer, using eight data lines. Serial ports are used for modems and for linking PC computers together into simple networks. These work one bit at a time, and at their simplest need only a single connection (and earth return) between the devices that are connected. Serial ports are seldom quite so simple, however.

- Modern motherboards carry one parallel and two serial ports on board, so that when a new motherboard is installed you have to fit connectors between the motherboard and the strip of metal that fits in a slot space and carries the external connectors. If you need an additional port (usually a parallel port) you have to fit this as a card, usually into an ISA slot.

Mouse ports are more specialized, used only for the mouse or its equivalent trackball or graphics digitizer. When you construct your own machine it is most unlikely that you will be able to lay your hands on a mouse port card unless you buy a mouse that has the card packaged with it. Some motherboards include a mouse port of the PS/2 type, others omit the mouse port. Since most computers have at least one unused serial port, it's usually cheaper to buy a serial mouse or other pointing device that uses the serial port. The keyboard port is always permanently fitted to the motherboard as distinct from being added in the form of a card. This can use the DIN or the PS/2 type of connector, and adapters are available if your keyboard does not use the same connector as the motherboard.

• ATX motherboards usually carry the PS/2 type of keyboard and mouse connectors.

The provision of one parallel and two serial ports, particularly on the motherboard, is simple and unlikely to cause problems. If, however, you want to use two parallel ports or three serial ports problems can arise because of conflicts of addresses and interrupts if you use older cards or an older motherboard.

The *address* for a port card means the code reference number that is used to locate the circuits on the card. By using this method, data can be sent to a port using much the same methods as when it is written to the memory by using a memory address number. A port needs to be able to use a unique address number because if two ports shared the same address there would have to be some additional method of determining which one is to be used.

The *interrupt* is a signal that the computer uses as a signal to divert its attention. If your computer is busy attending to the keys that you are pressing, and a port needs to input data, an interrupt signal from the port will cause the computer to suspend servicing the keyboard. It will then turn its attention (by running a different routine) to servicing the port, reading in or writing out the data. When this has been done, the earlier routine is resumed where it left off, and the break is often quite undetected. Each interrupt needs to use a code number to indicate which device has interrupted the action and so trigger the correct routine to service the interrupt. An interrupt is the way in which a port can make use of the computer without the need to shut down programs. Once again, conflicts of interrupts can cause port problems that can be difficult to resolve.

The signals that are used to synchronize the computer to the needs of whatever is connected to the port are called 'handshaking' signals. A typical handshaking sequence might consist of a computer sending out the 'are you ready?' signal through the port to the printer or other device. This will continue until the other device sends back a 'yes, ready' signal. Data will then be sent until the remote device sends a 'hang on' signal, and the flow of data will be halted until this signal is removed. The word 'handshaking' emphasizes the interaction that is needed, requiring more than one transmission of control signals between computer and remote device. Another term for the same sort of thing is 'flow control' and you are likely to meet with both of these phrases when you deal with communications hardware and software.

The parallel port – principles

The parallel port is often termed a Centronics port because its standardized format is due to the printer manufacturers Centronics which devised this form of port in the 1970s. The PC Centronics port uses a 25-pin D-type female connector at the PC end of the cable, and the 36-pin Amphenol type at the printer end. These connectors are illustrated in Figure 5.1, and the corresponding pins are:

Signal	DB-25	36-pin	Signal	DB-25	36-pin
Strobe	1	1	D0	2	2
D1	3	3	D2	4	4
D3	5	5	D4	6	6
D5	7	7	D6	8	8
D7	9	9	Ackn	10	10
Busy	11	11	PE	12	12
Slct	13	13	Auto	14	14
Error	15	32	Reset/Init	16	31
Slct In	17	36	Earth	18–25	16, 19–30, 33
NC	15, 18, 34				

The D0 to D7 signals are the eight data lines, and the direction is always out *from* the computer. When an older type of parallel connector is used for two-way data communication, four of the data lines are used for the outward signals and four of the control pins are used for the input signals. This makes the use of a parallel port

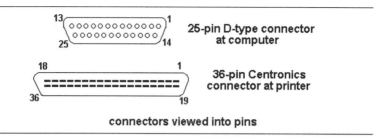

5.1 The printer parallel cable connections.

for two-way communication rather slower than the use of the signals on the slots, so you should use a parallel-port disk drive, for example, only if the installation of an internal drive is impossible.

- Many types of printers now use software control to a greater extent, allowing the manufacturer to dispense with a control panel on the printer itself. This is possible only if all the lines in the connector can be used for two-way (bidirectional) signals, and this type of cable is distinguished by the lettering on its outer covering that reads *IEEE STD 1284-1994 compliant*. If your printer needs a bidirectional cable, this is the type that must be used.

In normal use, each data pin has its own earth pin, and the connecting wires are a twisted pair for each, so minimizing interference between lines. The control signals are as follows, taking an input as meaning a signal into the computer from the printer, and an output as a signal from the computer to the printer.

- Note that printer manuals use the opposite sense for input and output.

Strobe is an active-low pulse output to the printer to gate the flow of a set of data signals on the D0–D7 lines. *Auto*, if used, is an output to the printer that, when held low, ensures that the paper is fed on by after printing a line. The *Reset/Init* signal output, active low, will cause the printer to be reset, clearing all data that might have been in the buffer memory of the printer. The *Slct In* output, also active low, inhibits all output to the printer unless this line is held low. Problems with 'dead' printers are often traced to this latter line being disconnected.

The remaining control signals are all inputs to the computer from the printer. The *Ackn* signal, active low, is a short pulse that acknowledges that data has been received at the printer and that the printer is ready for another byte. The *Busy* line is active high to indicate that data cannot be sent because the printer cannot accept it. The *PE* input indicates that the printer is out of paper, and *Slct* is active high to indicate that the printer is selected for use (the printer is on-line). The *Error* input, active low, signals that the printer is off-line, that the paper-end detector has operated, or that the printer is jammed (paper or ribbon, for example) and cannot operate.

Fitting an extra parallel port card

The parallel port is normally part of the motherboard, and is configured to be the port designated as LPT1, the main printer port, also designated as PRN. This means that it will use an address of 03BCh or 0378h and an interrupt number which is normally 7. The address and interrupt numbers are always quoted in a scale of 16 (hexadecimal scale), using letters A to F for the ordinary numbers 10 to 15. The letter 'h' following the number is a reminder that this is a hexadecimal number. See Appendix C for details of hexadecimal numbers.

The reason for the alternative address codes is that some graphics cards and chipsets make use of the address code 3BCh for their own purposes. Currently, these makes are Matrox, ATI mach64, TBLMB Horizon, STB2MB Powergraph. If you have any of these, the LPT1 port will be forced to use the address of 0378h (which is normally allocated to LPT1 on older machines). Other graphics cards may in the future make use of this address, so that you need to allow for this when a parallel port card is installed by allowing Windows to detect the new hardware and allocated the addresses and interrupt numbers.

If you install a second parallel port, you will normally make this LPT2 by using the address 0278h and the interrupt number 5. There may be problems in installing an LPT3 port if you have any of the video cards or chipsets noted above, because this port would normally use the 03BCh address. These selections of address number and interrupt (IRQ) number are usually made on a parallel port card by setting jumpers. Modern port cards that conform to the Windows Plug and Play (PnP) system have no jumpers and are set automatically by Windows.

- You should always use the Windows *Add Hardware* option of Control Panel if you put in other ports, so that conflicts can be avoided. This applies both to old cards that use jumpers (with the jumpers correctly set) and to later PnP cards.

Add-on units that make use of a parallel port usually are of the 'feed-through' variety, which means that the plug that engages with the printer socket carries a socket on its back. The printer can be plugged into this socket and used normally because the operating system can control the port so as to distinguish its dual uses. You should not attempt to stack several such add-ons, however. In some cases the connection cannot be made feed-through and the best solution is to add another port. One example is a scanner which can be used along with the printer as a copier. Sharing a port during this action would lead to conflicts.

A printer is not necessarily made useful simply by connecting it up to a port. Before you can print anything much with it you need to install printer drivers, though there are some items that you can print using MS-DOS. I shall assume that you are more likely to be printing from Windows.

Serial ports – principles

The serial transfer of data makes use of only one line (plus a ground return) for data, with the data being transmitted one bit at a time at a strictly controlled rate. The standard system is known as RS-232, and has been in use for a considerable time with machines such as teleprinters, so that a lot of features of RS-232 seem pointless as applied to modern equipment. When RS-232 was originally specified, two types of device were used and were classed as Data Terminal Equipment (DTE) and as Data Communications Equipment (DCE). A DTE device can send out or receive serial signals, and is a terminal in the sense that the signals are not routed elsewhere. A DCE device is a half-way house for signals, like a modem (see later, this chapter) which converts serial data signals into tones for communication over telephone lines or converts received tones into digital signals. Because the serial port is so closely associated with the use of a serial mouse the information is also covered here. The use of a modem is covered in Chapter 7.

The original concept of RS-232 was that a DTE device would always be connected to a DCE device. With the development of microcomputers and the use of parallel rather than serial ports for printers it is now just as common to require to connect two DTE devices to each other, such as one computer to another computer. This means that the connections in the cable must be changed, as we shall see. The original specification also stipulated that DTE equipment would use a male connector (plug) and the DCE equipment would use a female (socket), but you are likely to find either gender of connector on either type of device nowadays. The problem of how connectors are wired up is one that we'll come back to several times in this chapter. What started as a simple and standardized system has now grown into total confusion, and this sort of problem occurs all the way along the communications trail, not least in the use of words.

The original cable specification of RS-232 was for a connecting cable of 25 leads, as shown in Figure 5.2. Many of these connections

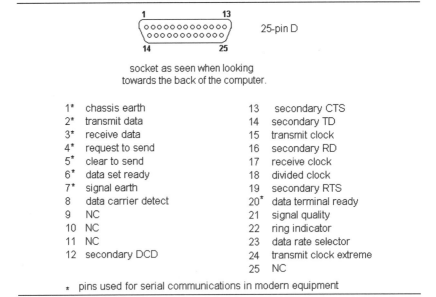

socket as seen when looking
towards the back of the computer.

1*	chassis earth	13	secondary CTS
2*	transmit data	14	secondary TD
3*	receive data	15	transmit clock
4*	request to send	16	secondary RD
5*	clear to send	17	receive clock
6*	data set ready	18	divided clock
7*	signal earth	19	secondary RTS
8	data carrier detect	20*	data terminal ready
9	NC	21	signal quality
10	NC	22	ring indicator
11	NC	23	data rate selector
12	secondary DCD	24	transmit clock extreme
		25	NC

* pins used for serial communications in modern equipment

5.2 The standard 25-pin form of RS-232 connector wiring.

9-pin D

socket as seen when looking
towards the back of the computer.

1   data carrier detect (DCD)
2   receive data (RX)
3   transmit data (TX)
4   data terminal ready (DTR)
5   signal earth
6   data set ready (DSR)
7   ready to send (RTS)
8   clear to send (CTS)
9   ring indicator (RI)

5.3   The modern 9-pin serial connector wiring.

reflect the use of old-fashioned telephone equipment and teleprinters, and very few applications of RS-232 now make use of more
than eight lines. The standard connector for PC machines is now
the D-type 9 pin, Figure 5.3, but even in this respect standards are
widely ignored and some manufacturers use quite different connectors. Worse still, some equipment in the past made use of the full
25-pin system, but used the 'spare' pins to carry other signals or
even DC supply lines. Modern computers have one of each type of
socket, using ports COM1 and COM2.

If any cables that you need are supplied along with the associated
card or equipment you have a better chance of getting things working than if you try to marry up a new piece of equipment with a
cable that has been taken from something else. The important
point is that you cannot go into a shop and ask for an RS-232
cable or a serial cable, because like the canned foods, RS-232
cables exist in 57 varieties. The advantages of using serial connections, however, outweigh the problems, because when a modem is
connected by the RS-232 cable to your computer you can use a
simple single line (telephone or radio link), and distance is no problem. Wherever you can telephone or send radio messages you can
transfer computer data provided that both transmitter and receiver
operated to the same standards. A huge variety of adapters (such

as gender changers) can be bought to ensure that your cable can be fitted to a socket that may not be of the correct variety, but this does not guarantee that the connections will be right.

All of this information may look academic, but the conclusion is practical enough. If you are going to join two computers that are in the same room or the same building and pass data between them, you need a serial cable which is described as non-modem, or DTE to DTE. If you are going to transfer data over telephone lines or radio links then you need a modem and a modem cable, or DTE to DCE cable. The good news is that if you use for your telephone line transfers the type of device that is referred to as an 'internal modem' you don't have to worry at all about this problem of using the correct cable. The differences are that the modem or DTE to DCE cable has corresponding pins connected, and the non-modem or null-modem type has several reversed connections, Figure 5.4.

- You may find difficulty nowadays in obtaining null-modem cables and will have to settle for using a modem cable along with an adapter for one end that reverses some of the connections.

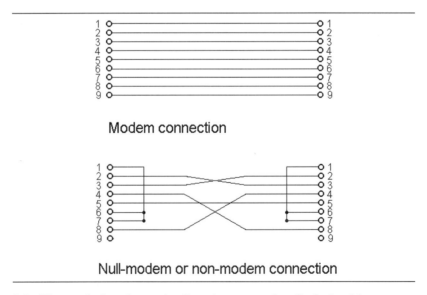

Modem connection

Null-modem or non-modem connection

5.4 The standard modem and null-modem connections for 9-pin wiring.

Setting up the serial port

The 25-pin serial connector on the computer is a male type to distinguish it from the 25-pin female connector that is used for the parallel port of the PC. The normal serial port arrangement on a modern motherboard is to provide two serial ports (one 9 pin and one 25 pin), referred to as COM1 and COM2.

The use of more than two serial ports is fraught with problems on older machines because a COM3 port, for example, had to share the IRQ4 interrupt with the COM1 port. This need not be a problem if only one port is ever used at a time. If you use the COM1 port for a mouse and the COM3 port for connection to another computer problems will certainly arise unless you can run software that allows the ports to share the interrupt correctly. This problem arose on older machines because the standard PC machine was not well provided with interrupt lines. Modern motherboards provide for the use of expansion cards for COM3 and COM4 without conflicts. For most users, however, two serial ports are quite sufficient, and these can be set as COM1 and COM2:

Port number	Address	Interrupt
COM1	03F8	IRQ4*
COM2	02F8	IRQ3*
COM3	03E8	IRQ2
COM4	02E8	IRQ5*

* Standard setting. The use of IRQ2 is not usually possible, and IRQ5 may not be available, depending on the setup of the machine.

The most common use for a serial port nowadays is to make use of a serial mouse, because when an internal modem (see Chapter 7) is fitted it normally contains its own serial port chip and does not require a cable attachment to a connector on the PC. An internal modem will normally contain a port that Windows will set up as COM3, but without any conflicts with COM1.

The mouse

The mouse, Figure 5.5, is another way in which information is fed into the computer, and for graphics and drawing (CAD) programs,

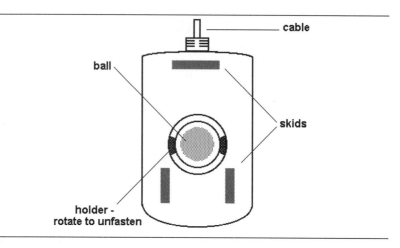

5.5 The underside of a typical mouse.

along with many DTP programs, is one of the really serious ways of working with such programs. The other options are trackballs and graphics tablets, and the graphics tablet is a better option for drawing work. A mouse or other pointer device is *essential* for using Windows. The mouse consists of a heavy metal ball, coated with a synthetic rubber skin, which can be rotated when the mouse is moved. The movement of the ball is transmitted to small rollers, Figure 5.6. It is then sensed in various ways, depending on the make of the mouse, such as magnetic changes, or by light reflection,

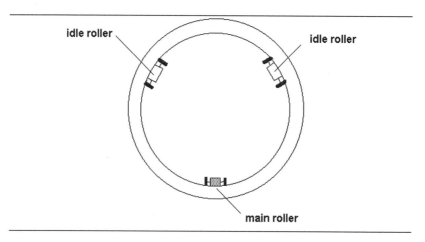

5.6 The rollers that are revealed when the ball is removed.

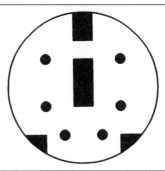

5.7 The shape of a PS/2 connector, often used for mouse and/or keyboard.

and the signals that indicate the movement are returned to the computer to be used in moving the cursor.

The mouse action depends on software being present, and this can cause a considerable amount of confusion. If you have bought and fitted a mouse independently of the manufacturer of the computer, follow closely the instructions that come with the mouse, and check that the mouse is the correct type for your computer. Windows will install the correct type of driver for your mouse if you allow it to detect the mouse as new hardware.

Some motherboards contain a mouse port, and this is usually of the PS/2 type which uses a small 6-pin connector, Figure 5.7. Another popular method is to use a serial mouse which plugs into the 9-pin serial port (usually COM2). Avoid buying a mouse that is intended for a specific make of computer, because this may be almost impossible to connect to a standard PC machine.

Mouse problems and solutions

MOUSE HAS NO EFFECT ON CURSOR

The usual reason is that the software is not installed. If Windows has not automatically detected your mouse and installed a driver you will have to try manual detection (use Control Panel – Add Hardware) and you may have to insert a floppy that contains a suitable Windows driver.

CURSOR MOVES IN THE WRONG DIRECTION

The mouse is not intended for the model of computer. This is a problem relating to a bus mouse, and you will need a wiring diagram for the mouse plug or socket. Either change the mouse or change over the connections at the mouse plug or make an adapter which has crossed-over connections for the mouse signals. If the reversal is horizontal only, reverse the connections marked as XA and XB. If the reversal is in the vertical direction only, reverse the YA and YB connections. Reverse both if both directions are reversed.

MOUSE JAMMED

Clean the ball, avoiding spirit solvents – spectacle lens cleaning fluid and a soft cloth are preferred. Also clean the rollers that you can see inside the mouse casing when the ball is removed. There are often three of these, two of which serve to locate the ball, with a third, spring loaded, transmitting the movement to a detector. These rollers are quite difficult to clean, The best way is to wrap some cloth (a handkerchief will do) around the points of tweezers, moisten this, and rub it across each roller. Move it sideways a few times, then pull or push to rotate the roller slightly and then rub it sideways again. Dirty rollers are a much more common source of trouble than a dirty ball.

ERRATIC MOVEMENT

When it becomes difficult to move a mouse precisely, the usual fault is a build-up of dirt on the rollers, see above, and a thorough cleaning will work wonders. If this does not restore normal operation, check for defective plug contacts and cable connections.

Games ports

A games port is often included as part of a sound card. There is no universal standard for such games ports, and no two seem to be identical in pin-out. The connections to the port refer to buttons and positions for connection to a joystick. Since a PC machine is intended for serious computing uses rather than games, the games port can be disabled. Figure 5.8 shows a typical pin arrangement for the games/joystick port, also used for MIDI signals, on a sound card.

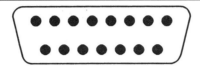

5.8   A typical 15-pin games or joystick port on a sound card.

USB and Firewire

USB is the abbreviation of Universal Serial Bus, a faster type of serial connection that is now being fitted to some motherboards. Devices that use USB can be chained so that one USB port on the motherboard could serve up to 127 external devices. The most recent application is from Philips in the form of loudspeakers that can accept the USB digital input, so that they can be used independently of a sound card. Windows 98 will recognize and use USB devices if you have any.

Firewire is another form of fast connection that can be daisy-chained from one device to another from a port on the computer. So far, it is not being used on motherboards because final specifications are not ready, but it is already used on some digital camcorders as a way of passing information out and, in some examples, in. Firewire cards are available to add to the computer using a PCI slot, and at the time of writing, the prices ranged from the acceptable to the ridiculous.

Chapter 6

Setting up

Once you have installed all the cards on the motherboard, whether you are working on a machine that you have constructed from scratch or improving an older machine you have bought, you should now turn your attention to the setup of the whole computer system. This is something that is often neglected, and by spending just a little more time at this stage you can make it all much easier for yourself later. The first point to consider is how you intend to locate all the separate sections that make up a PC. When you are first testing your handiwork, the sections should all be accessible, and the monitor is best placed temporarily on one side of the main casing.

The conventional format for a flip-lid desktop case is to place the monitor on top of the main casing, with the keyboard in front and the mouse to one side. This places the weight of the monitor on top of the lid of the case. If the monitor is a heavy one, as all colour monitors are, you should spread the weight with a square of plywood or chipboard placed between monitor and case, so that the edges of the case are taking the weight rather than the more vulnerable lid. This arrangement, though very popular, does not allow you to flip open the lid without first moving the monitor, and a much better arrangement is to place the main casing on a separate shelf, preferably under the desk or table. An old coffee table of the low variety can be used, and if there is enough clearance above the main case this allows you to flip open the lid without the need to shift anything. This is a much more suitable arrangement if you are likely to be making frequent changes to cards and other aspects of the interior of the machine.

● The popularity of the tower form of construction, particularly the mini or midi tower, is due to the small *footprint* it makes on a desk. A tower can sit on the edge of a desk, allowing the monitor and keyboard to be arranged more centrally; an alternative is to place the main tower under the desk – this is essential for a full-size tower which would be too large on a desktop.

You can place the mouse to the left or to the right, and software will allow you to interchange the functions of the mouse switches to allow for left-hand or right-hand use. Both mouse and keyboard normally come with leads that are long enough to give you considerable choice in where you place them relative to the main casing.

Wiring

The standard form of power supply that is used in the PC has a Eurosocket connector that is intended for the power to the monitor or the printer; sometimes both can be connected. This supply may be separately fused inside the power supply unit, or it may share the mains fuse in the 3-pin mains plug of the computer. Some monitors are provided with a Euroconnector, but if none is provided, you can connect your own, Figure 6.1. Euroconnectors are available from the main electronics supply firms such as Maplin and RS Components (ElectroComponents). Remember that the Euroconnector you use for a monitor power lead should be the cable-end pin type to match the socket type used on the computer. The exposed pins of the connector must never be connected to a mains plug. The Euroconnector can be obtained as cable fitting (plug) or as chassis fitting (socket), and either form can be male or female.

If you have several auxiliary units such as powered loudspeakers, a scanner, a low-consumption printer, etc., you may want all of these to be switched on and off with the computer. This is particularly important now that so many items come without a separate

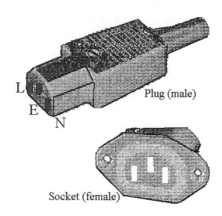

L
E
N
Plug (male)

Socket (female)

6.1 The standard Euroconnector. Use the female version for the mains side of a lead and the male version for the dead side.

mains switch. You can solve this by making up a socket strip that is fitted with a Europlug in place of a 13 A mains plug. The Europlug can be inserted into the power outlet of the computer, and you can plug in the monitor and your other auxiliaries into the extension sockets. This ensures that when you switch the computer off, everything is off. The only thing to watch is that you do not exceed the current rating of the Euroconnector at the computer. This is seldom stated, and you should assume that it is no more than 3 amps.

- You can now buy socket strips with individual switches. These are particularly useful for connecting devices that have no separate mains switch, such as some makes of printers and scanners.

The power cable to the main casing will use another Euroconnector, and you will normally have to fit a mains plug. This must be a standard UK 3-pin plug, and the fuse *must* be a 3 A type. Do *not* on any account fit a 13 A fuse, because the internal cabling of the machine is not rated to take such a current without serious damage. If a plug has been supplied, check the fuse rating for yourself, even if you have been assured that it is a 3 A type. At this stage, do not insert the mains plug.

To connect up the units, you need complete access to the rear of the main case – do not try to insert connectors by feel. The keyboard

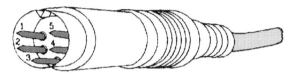

1	Clock pulse
2	Earth
3	Data
4	+5V
5	Not used

6.2 The standard form of DIN keyboard plug. Adapters are available to convert to PS/2 plug fittings.

connector should be inserted first. This is usually a rather fragile DIN plug, Figure 6.2, and its socket is directly mounted on the motherboard. The alternative on some motherboards is the PS/2 type of plug which is even smaller, see Figure 5.7. Locate the key for the plug, and try to use the minimum force when inserting it, because the socket on the motherboard is not particularly rugged. If the plug does not slide easily into the socket, stop and try to find out why – you may be trying to put the plug in with the pins turned to the wrong angle. The keyboard cable is usually coiled, and if it does not stretch far enough in its coiled form, pull it out a bit. You can buy cable extenders if needed.

A keyboard can be easily replaced in the course of an upgrade, though there is seldom any need to do so unless you are working on a very old machine with the 83-key arrangement. Do not worry about having a keyboard whose plug does not match the motherboard socket, because you can buy DIN-to-PS/2 and PS/2-to-DIN adapters.

The mouse can now be connected, either to its mouse port if it is the bus type of mouse, or to a serial port. Remember that both serial and parallel ports can use the same form of 25-pin D-connector, but the parallel port uses a female socket. If you have a 9-pin connector on the COM2 port, use this for a serial mouse. The connectors that are used for this port can normally be screwed into place, but do not screw them down when you are first testing. Drape the mouse cable to one side of the keyboard, leaving enough slack to allow you to move the mouse easily.

Now connect the monitor, inserting the Euroconnector into the PC (female) socket, or plugging in to a mains power point if you have opted to keep the monitor separate from the PC supply. The monitor data plug then has to be inserted. The standard type of 15-pin monitor D-plug will fit only one way round, and even for testing purposes it is advisable to fasten the plug into the socket using the screws at the side. The data cable for a monitor is usually thick, because it uses several sets of twisted leads, and it is also stiff because of metal shielding, so that the connector is likely to be pulled out if you move the monitor unless the plug is fastened in.

- Note that the monitor plug uses three rows of pins, unlike the 15-pin games port plug.

Using CMOS-RAM setup

The PC keeps some data stored in CMOS RAM memory, backed up by a small battery that is located on the motherboard. Some motherboards provide for an external battery to be used either together with or in place of this internal one, and if you encounter problems such as a request to alter the CMOS RAM setup each time you boot the machine, battery failure is the most likely cause. If you have constructed or altered a machine, particularly if you have installed a hard drive, you are likely to get a message when you boot to the effect that an unrecognized hard drive is being used. Along with this you will be asked to press a key to start the CMOS setup. This type of message is delivered when the machine senses that there is a discrepancy between what is stored in the CMOS RAM and what is physically present, but minor changes such as adding ports will not necessarily affect the CMOS RAM.

- Older machines used a nickel-cadmium rechargeable battery on the motherboard, but this has now changed in favour of a single lithium cell, which is more compact and has a longer life. Do not attempt to measure the voltage of this cell (nominally 3 V) using an old-fashioned voltmeter because a conventional voltmeter will take more current from the cell than the CMOS RAM does, and will shorten its life. If you must check the lithium cell, use a digital voltmeter.

If you do not get a CMOS RAM setup notice when you boot, you may see a notice on the screen notifying you that you can press a key in order to get into the CMOS setup. The way that is used to make the machine run its Setup depends on the make of chips that it uses (the chipset). One common method, used with AMI BIOS machines, is to offer you a short interval in which pressing the Del key on the keypad (at the right-hand side of the keyboard) will enter Setup. Some AWARD chipset machines require you to press a set of keys, Ctrl-Alt-Esc in this interval. Whatever key or key combination is to be used, it should be noted in the documentation for the motherboard, and also on the screen when you start up the computer. Note that pressing the *Delete* key (in the set of six above the cursor keys) as distinct from the Del key will have no effect – this is because the machine is at this stage being controlled by a very small program in the ROM which allows only very limited capabilities.

The snag is that if, as recommended, you have wired your monitor to the Euroconnector so that it is switched on by the computer, the monitor may not have warmed up in time to display the message. Colour monitors in particular tend to miss the message because they warm up slowly. The remedy is to boot up in the usual way, and when the monitor is fully active, press the Ctrl-Alt-Del key combination. Use the Ctrl and Alt keys to the left of the spacebar, and the Del key on the keypad at the right. This key combination causes what is called a *warm boot*, meaning that the computer restarts (clearing its memory on the way), but omits some self-test routines so that the restart is faster. During this restart you should see a message such as:

WAIT...

Hit <DEL> If you want to run Setup

– the AMI BIOS message is illustrated here.

Whichever method is used, it should be possible to see a display such as that in Figure 6.3. This is a simplified example of a modern Award BIOS and chipset display and those for other machines will differ in detail. The important point is that you are offered a set of optional menus to choose from, of which the first (already selected) is by far the most important at this stage. Until you are thoroughly familiar with the system, do not attempt to use any menus other

```
                    STANDARD CMOS SETUP


                  ADVANCED CMOS SETUP
                  ADVANCED CHIPSET SETUP
          AUTO CONFIGURATION WITH BIOS DEFAULTS
          AUTO CONFIGURATION WITH POWER-ON DEFAULTS
                   CHANGE PASSWORD
                  HARD DISK UTILITY
                WRITE TO CMOS AND EXIT
             DO NOT WRITE TO CMOS AND EXIT
```

6.3 A typical main menu for CMOS RAM setup.

than the Standard CMOS Setup. The only exception is that if you find the system misbehaving after a change in the CMOS setup you can recover by entering the Setup again and selecting the Setup Defaults. The BIOS setup reminds you of this when you opt to use either of the main Setup menus.

This main menu contains the Password options to allow you to create a password either for *Supervisor* or *User* or both. Passwording can be useful when a machine is available to a large number of people, but unless you have security problems it is best to avoid passwording. For one thing, you need to remember your own password(s). If a password is easy to remember, it is usually easy for someone else to guess. If you forget a password you will be locked out of your own machine and there is no simple way then of disabling the passwording, though it can be done by an expert. If you are desperate, some varieties of AMI BIOS provide for the password changing to AMI when the backup battery is discharged or momentarily disconnected. Another option on other boards is to change over a jumper to clear the CMOS RAM by disconnecting the battery. Find out for yourself how to reset a forgotten password if you decide to use this form of protection. Note that you may have to re-enter CMOS RAM information after this action.

When you opt for the Standard setup, you will see a display that is, typically, illustrated in Figure 6.4, and the important point is that the information on the drive types should be present. Any alteration in the installed drives has to be notified, otherwise the

```
Date (mn/date/year) : Sun, Oct 03 1993              Base Memory : 640 KB
Time (hour/min/sec) : 10  :  47  :  12              Ext. memory : 4096 KB
Daylight saving     : Disabled      Cyln  Head  WPcom  LZone   Sect   Size
Hard Disk C: type   : 47 = USER TYPE 1001   15     0      0     17   125 MB
Hard Disk D: type   : Not Installed
Floppy drive A:     : 1.44 MB, 3½"
Floppy drive B:     : 1.2 MB, 5¼"            Sun  Mon  Tue  Wed  Thu  Fri  Sat
Primary Display     : VGA/PGA/EGA            26   27   28   29   30    1    2
Keyboard            : Installed               3    4    5    6    7    8    9
                                             10   11   12   13   14   15   16
Month               : Jan, Feb, . . . Dec    17   18   19   20   21   22   23
Date                : 01, 02, 03, . . . 31   24   25   26   27   28   29   30
Year                :11981, 1982, . . . 2099 31    1    2    3    4    5    6

ESC: Exit  Arrow keys: Select  F2/F3 : Color PU/PD : Modify
```

6.4 A typical Standard CMOS setup page, showing the important HARD DISKS section. The memory size is notified here also – the illustration shows 64 Mbyte of RAM.

CMOS RAM Setup table is likely to be presented to you each time you boot. If you have constructed a machine from scratch, or altered the drives of an older machine, you will certainly need to alter the particulars shown here. Altering a line of information is, typically, done by using the arrow keys (cursor keys) to move the cursor to the item(s) you want to change, and pressing either the *Page Up* or *Page Down* keys to change the item. Note that you cannot type in numbers or day names, only cycle through the options that are provided. What is less clear is how to find and enter the information about the hard drive that you need to supply to the system. At this stage in its action, the computer cannot make use of the mouse, and only a few keys, such as the cursor and Esc keys, are recognized.

The important section is headed HARD DISKS, and there are columns labelled TYPE, SIZE, CYLS, HEAD, PRECOMP, LANDZ, SECTOR and MODE. The list under the HARD DISKS column contains Primary Master, Primary Slave, Secondary Master and Secondary Slave, and each line that is filled in corresponds to a device. Normally, you will use the Primary Master line for a hard drive and Secondary Master for a CD-ROM drive. The information in the other columns will either be read automatically from a new drive, or can be filled in from the information supplied with the hard drive.

The usual method of forcing the computer to recognize the hard drive is to select Auto as the TYPE, so that the drive will be recognized the next time you boot the computer. Another method is to use the option in the main menu of IDE HDD AUTO DETECTION. If you need to use manual entry for any reason (an older hard drive, usually) then moving the cursor to the Primary Master line allows you to use the *Page Up* and *Page Down* keys to alter the setting to USER. You can then fill in figures for your own hard drive.

This is not helpful if you have just acquired an IDE drive of unknown specification from a car-boot sale (should you have such a trusting nature?) and you want to use it. Laying aside the matter of buying technical products in such a way, not to mention the question mark that must hang over their origin if the seller cannot tell you anything about the drive, you can generally set up the drive by using Windows. If the drive is to PnP standard then the *Add New Hardware* option of Control Panel will allow Windows to detect the drive and set up the CMOS RAM correctly for it. There would be little point in buying a drive that is not to PnP standard, because it would be old and of inadequate size.

- Unless your hard drive is recognized correctly in the CMOS RAM settings it will probably not operate correctly – you might find that at best its capacity was incorrectly recorded; at worst that it did not retain data.

FLOPPY AND DISPLAY DETAILS

Once the hard drive details have been entered you must fill in the portion of the Setup form that deals with the floppy drives. Place the cursor on the line for *Drive A* and use the *Page Up* and *Page Down* keys until you see the type of drive you have installed, usually a 3.5″ 1.44 MB type – note that this counts 1 MB = 1000 KB rather than 1024 KB. There is a *Not Installed* option which is used for machines that are part of a network and which do not need disk drives – this might be the selected option if you have obtained a motherboard from a networked machine or you are refurbishing such a machine. It is also a simple way of preventing a casual user of the computer from inserting a floppy and loading in software that contains a virus. A knowledgeable user would know how to change the CMOS RAM setting (though you can protect this using a password, see later). The *Drive B* option is seldom needed.

The display line is selected in the same way. The normal option is VGA/EGA, whether you use a colour or a monochrome VGA monitor. There may be a *Not Installed* option that would be used for server machines on a network, and, as before, if you are refurbishing such a machine or using its motherboard you might find this option set. In this type of BIOS you have options for Halt On, specifying the kind of errors that will prevent the boot action from proceeding, and the usual option is *All Errors*. Other options are *No Errors, All but Keyboard, All but Diskette* and *All but Disk/Key*. The *All Errors* option is the default and you should not change this unless you know what you are doing.

You can then go back to the start of the list to correct the calendar and clock details if necessary. The calendar details are usually correct unless the board was not set up correctly initially, or the battery has failed, but the clock may be a few minutes out. The clock and calendar will probably need to be set from scratch if you are using a new motherboard and the CMOS RAM has been cleared. You are not obliged to set the calendar and clock at this stage, but it is useful to do so. If you want to correct the time later it can be done using the Windows Date and Time controls rather than by using the CMOS-RAM option.

- Note that any new motherboard that you buy after reading this book will contain a BIOS ROM that allows for the year 2000. If you are in doubt, you can download a free diagnostic program from the Web site:

  http://www.y2000fix.com/Diagnostic.html

This provides a short file called diagnose.exe which can be copied to the C:\ root drive of your computer and expanded to give the set of diagnostic programs that includes TEST2000.EXE.

Booting up

You can now leave the CMOS setup program, taking the option to *Write to CMOS and Exit,* and when you boot the machine the hard drive should now be recognized. If you are using a hard drive that has been in service, it may be provided with MS-DOS. If this is so, you should see the message:

Loading MS-DOS...

(or something similar) appear, and hear the disk working hard. You may find other items of software on the disk. Sometimes a new hard drive comes ready for use in this way, though it is more normal to require formatting. If instead of the Loading MS-DOS message you get a message such as:

Error loading operating system
OR
Non-system disk or disk error

then the hard drive is almost certainly not formatted.

Using FDISK

FDISK is an old type of program that at one time seemed obsolete because hard drives were once supplied with the FDISK action (disk partitioning) already carried out. You may, however, find that a new large-capacity hard drive is supplied without partitioning so that you must use FDISK. You will need a modern (FAT32) version of FDISK such as is included with Windows 98, or use software supplied by the manufacturer or retailer of the hard drive.

Start the computer with the MS-DOS system disk in the floppy drive, and wait until the prompt A:> appears. Now type the command:

FDISK

– and press the ENTER or RETURN key. You will see a display that includes the lines:

Current fixed disk drive: 1

Choose one of the following:

1. Create DOS partition or Logical DOS Drive
2. Set active partition
3. Delete partition or Logical DOS drive

4. Display partition information
5. Change current fixed disk drive
    Enter choice: [5]
    Press ESC to exit FDISK

If you are setting up the one and only hard drive, use option 1, but if you are setting up a second hard drive use option 5 to select your slave drive. This option 5 will show the drive details for both drives so that you can select which one to partition. Once the drive is selected, the display returns and you can choose option 1. You will be asked if you want to set the whole drive as a single partition, and for a modern computer you should answer Y to this question. The partitioning action will be carried out, and you can press the ESC key until the system reboots.

You can then use the MS-DOS system disk in Drive A to format the hard drive. For a single master drive, the command is:

FORMAT C:

– and press the ENTER or RETURN key. For a second hard drive, you will probably use D: as the drive letter, so that your command becomes FORMAT D:. If you are formatting a slave drive be very careful that you do not reformat your main (master) drive instead.

A new hard drive is not usually provided with Windows 98 pre-installed unless you have specifically asked for this and paid for it, so that once you have MS-DOS working you can proceed to install Windows. You should now test that you can boot from the (master) hard drive by taking out the floppy system disk and rebooting. If your CMOS-RAM setup allows you the option of booting from the hard drive directly without checking the floppy drive, take this option.

CMOS BIOS Setup

You would not normally use the CMOS BIOS Setup section when you were first booting up a new or refurbished machine, but for future reference it is useful to know what this part of the Setup can accomplish. The difficulty here is that there is no standard set of actions, and the examples are taken from an Award BIOS. Others

Typematic Rate Programming	: Disabled	Adapter ROM Shadow D800, 32K	: Disabled
Typematic Rate Delay (ms)	: 250	Adapter ROM Shadow E000, 32K	: Disabled
Typematic Rate (Char/sec)	: 30.0	Adapter ROM Shadow E800, 32K	: Disabled
Above 1MB Memory Test	: Disabled	System ROM Shadow F000, 64K	: Disabled
Memory Test Tick Sound	: Disabled	Memory Wait States	: Disabled
Memory Parity Error Check	: Disabled	RAS Time Out	: Enabled
HIT <ESC> Message Display	: Disabled	16bit ISA Cycle Insert Wait	: 0 ms
Hard Disk Type 47 Data Area	: 0:300	RAS Active Timer Insert Wait	: Disabled
Wait for <F1> If Any Error	: Disabled	Quick RAS Precharge Time	: Disabled
System Boot Up NUM Lock	: On	Slow Refresh	: Enabled
Numeric Processor	: Absent	IO Recover Period Define	: Disabled
Floppy Drive Seek at Boot	: Disabled		
System Boot Up Sequence	: C:, A:		
Internal Cache Memory	: Disabled		
Password Checking Option	: Disabled		
Video ROM Shadow C000, 32K	: Disabled		
Adapter ROM Shadow C800, 32K	: Disabled		
Adapter ROM Shadow D000, 32K	: Disabled		

6.5 A typical CMOS BIOS Setup page.

are likely to differ, though several important options will be the same. Some of these options can be used without the need for deeper understanding of the computer, but those which deal with memory allocations, particularly with ROM shadowing (see later) should be left strictly alone until you know what is involved on your machine. A typical list is shown in Figure 6.5.

The first item is *Virus Warning*. This protects the parts of a hard drive (boot sector and FAT) that can be damaged by a virus, and the default setting is *Disabled*. This is because you cannot load an operating system (DOS or Windows) without modifying these parts of the hard drive. You can set this to *Enabled* after Windows has been installed, but you will need to disable it again if you upgrade your Windows software.

The two following items deal with *Internal* and *External cache*, meaning memory that is used as a temporary store for the microprocessor. These should both be set to *Enabled*, because the speed of the machine will be noticeably lower if you disable either of these. The Quick Power On Self Test should be enabled to make booting faster by eliminating excessive testing. This is a hangover from the time when memory was considered unreliable.

The *HDD Sequence* option is a feature of the AWARD BIOS, and it allows you to choose whether to use the IDE hard drive to boot from or to use a SCSI drive.

The *Boot Sequence* line has the default of C;A and this will cause the machine to boot from the hard drive, using a floppy only if the hard drive cannot be used. This is a useful default, and you can change it to A;C if you want to test the machine without using the hard drive. Along with this, you can disable the action of seeking the floppy drive so that the machine does not activate the drive needlessly at each boot. Another floppy option is to allow the floppy to be used for reading only (default is read/write).

The *IDE HDD Block Mode Sectors* option is set by default at *HDD MAX* for modern hard drives, and this provides optimum performance. Other settings can be used for older drives.

Security Option decides when you need to enter a password if you have opted for this. The default is *System*, prompting for the password on each boot. The alternative is *Setup*, when a password is needed only when the CMOS Setup is used. These settings are used only if you have opted to use Passwording.

The *PS/2 Mouse Function Control* is normally set to *Auto*, allowing the system to detect the use of a PS/2 mouse automatically at boot time. This can be disabled if you use a serial mouse, so releasing the IRQ12 interrupt. The *PCI/VGA Palette Snoop* is usually disabled, but can be enabled if a non-standard graphics or video card shows colours incorrectly. The *OS/2 Onboard Memory > 64M* item is also disabled by default. You can enable it if you are using the OS/2 operating system with more than 64 Mbyte of memory. This indicates that there is no advantage in using more than 64 Mbyte of memory unless you are also using the OS/2 operating system.

BIOS shadowing means that the data in the BIOS ROM will be copied to RAM at boot time, because RAM is faster than ROM. The default is to enable this for the Video ROM, but you should not enable the other shadow options unless you know that you are using cards that contain ROM addresses in the six other ranges illustrated.

The *System Boot up Num Lock Status* option should be enabled, so that the number keypad on the right-hand side of the keyboard is set for numbers rather than its optional cursor keys. This avoids the need to have to press the Num Lock key after booting. The *Boot Up System Speed* setting is *High* by default and should not be altered.

Another set of BIOS options deals with the *Typematic rate*. This is the rate at which a key action will repeat when a key is held down, and there are two factors, the time delay between pressing a key and starting the repeat action, and the rate at which the key action repeats once it has started. The Setup options are to enable or disable the Typematic action, to set the delay, and to set the repeat rate. Typical default values are to have the action disabled, the delay set to a long 500 milliseconds (0.5 second) and the rate to a fast 150 characters per second. The time and rate settings have no effect if the Typematic action is disabled. Since Windows will override these settings and impose its own, there is no point in making the settings unless you plan to type data into MS-DOS programs.

THE NO-GO AREAS

The Chipset Features set of the AWARD BIOS should be left at default settings unless you know what you are doing and have the necessary information such as the response time of DRAM. You should also be careful about using the Power Management options, and keep the default settings if you are in doubt. Just because an option appears in one of these sets does not mean that your motherboard can cope with it. It is reasonable to use the action that shuts down the hard drive after a period of inactivity, but only if you are using a modern version of Windows that supports power management features of this type.

Bus mastering

Modern computers feature bus mastering, meaning that data can be transferred to and from hard drives and CD-ROM drives at a high speed without the need to make use of the main processor. This system is also called DMA, direct memory access, and its use can be detected in Windows Control Panel, see later. Modern hard drives use a version referred to as Ultra DMA.

Not all motherboards see to this automatically, and you may have to use a floppy disk containing bus-mastering software. For some motherboards, this can be run only after Windows has been installed, and you will have to check with the documentation that you have. It is very important to use bus mastering, because in its absence the computer will run at a much slower rate than you would expect after upgrading.

Chapter 7

Upgrading

This chapter is intended particularly for the reader who has taken or wants to take the simple and cost-effective route to a modern PC – upgrading an older machine. The machine may be one that you have had for some time, an old 80386 or 80486 machine, for example. It may be one that has been bought at a very low price at auction or in a car-boot sale (where machines recovered from skips outside hospitals or offices often end up). Another route for the upgrader is to buy a new machine which is at a rock-bottom price because it contains the essentials of a case, power supply and motherboard only. There are few suppliers of such machines nowadays, but the prices for such machines are lower than you would have to pay if you bought the parts and assembled them for yourself.

Machines bought at auctions, particularly from bankrupt office firms, can present you with an interesting gamble. Some of these are likely to be very powerful machines, particularly if a network has been in use and you can lay your hands on the server machine. You can also find fast and efficient networked machines with no disk drives, but with a fast processor and a lot of memory. You have to be able to look inside the cases for yourself and determine, from the processor type number and the number of SIMMs you can see, whether a machine is likely to be a bargain or not. Do not depend on an auctioneer's description, because they are not computer experts and have to rely in turn on whatever description they can find. Goods bought at auction are usually bought 'as seen' with no form of warranty as to content or origin.

In general, if a machine has the Pentium MMX or Pentium-2 chip on its motherboard and 16 Mbyte or more of memory, it will be snapped up by a dealer who can refurbish it and resell. You are not likely to get the chance to buy it cheaply for yourself. That said, a small local auction may not attract any dealers who know what to look for, and you can be very fortunate. The usual bargains at the larger auctions are the 80486DX and older Pentium machines, and if you can find one with a decent amount of memory and a hard drive, then it's no hardship to part with £100 or less, which is as little as you should need to secure it. Do not consider an 80486 machine unless it has a very large hard drive because it can be useful only after a new motherboard and fast EDO memory has been installed, and probably also a fast PCI graphics board. A machine with a large hard drive will almost certainly use SCSI, and you should ask yourself if you want to be tied to this system for other drives. Another point to consider is that the memory is unlikely to be of the modern fast EDO type, and the local bus on a pre-Pentium machine will be VLB, assuming that there is any local bus.

- This need not put you off if you can get a machine at a really low price, because a sum of about £180 should get you a good motherboard, 166MMX Pentium and a CD-ROM drive. If the machine has a large hard drive or pair of hard drives, it will be pretty competent even if the graphics board is slower than modern types.
- Do not consider 80386 or older machines, because these will require new *everything* to bring them up to date (and some of them are almost impossible to upgrade). Do not pay silly prices (£200 or more) for 80486 machines because by the time you have upgraded you will have spent more than you would pay for a new Pentium machine.

Even some modern machines, usually bearing famous names, are difficult to upgrade, which is why they found their way to the auction in the first place. Read all of this chapter before you consider this path to a new PC, because trying to upgrade some machines could be more expensive than starting from scratch. Avoid in particular machines with plastic, or very slim metal, cases. Avoid any whose drives are stamped with the same name as is on the case – a standard drive might not fit in the same space. Some famous-name machines came from manufacturers who made their own mother-boards and ensured that the standard types could not be fitted. If the name on the case is unfamiliar you are more likely to be in luck. Machines which use unfamiliar layouts should be avoided – they are likely to be good machines for their age, but upgrading them will be costly and difficult. It helps if you keep a note of the dimensions of a modern motherboard and you can check that this is much the same as the board inside a computer that looks like a bargain.

Drive change

One common upgrade route starts with the machine that has no hard drive, and sometimes no floppy drive, because it has been used as a workstation on a network. Another is the machine which uses a totally inadequate hard drive – though you can use a hard drive of as little as 120 Mbyte to run Windows 98 and Word in mini-mal form, there really is not enough room to install much else. Re-member that you have to avoid machines that use an old 5.25″ floppy drive, and old hard drives (other than SCSI types) are unli-kely to be useful. They will be too small to start with, and they are also likely to have just too many miles on the clock for comfort. Un-like electronic parts, hard drives are mechanical devices that will wear out in the course of time.

The comments in Chapter 3 apply to drive installation in general, and what follows is aimed particularly at the user who is stripping out an old drive or adding a drive to an older casing, rather than in-stalling a new drive into a new case. Obviously, the methods of in-stalling and using a drive are the same. What you need to look out for are machines of eccentric design and with unorthodox fastenings. Nameless clones are a delight to work on, because they follow a well-worn standard pattern. Big-name machines can be a night-mare, because only their own spare parts will fit, and these parts are usually three times as expensive as the (almost identical) part for the nameless clone.

The most pressing need for a drive occurs when the machine is a diskless workstation, or a workstation machine that has only a floppy drive. These machines have been networked to a very fast and larger server machine which provided the hard drive capacity and printer port for the separate workstations, but you often find that each workstation has a fast processor and plenty memory (allowing programs to be downloaded and run locally). The only thing to watch out for is that the casing is standard, providing three or more drive bays. Some workstations use an ultra-slimline casing which has no space for drives of any description, and this would not be a good buy even at a very low price unless you fancy starting from scratch with a new case, preferably an ATX case that has power leads for an AT type of board. If you have to buy a new case and motherboard, think what else you need to buy and ask yourself how this compares with a new machine of the same specification.

- Remember the adage about horses for courses. If your aim is to make a spare or second computer, then you need not be so fussy about keeping up to modern standards or how future-proof you are going to make it.

On a diskless machine, check that the power supply unit has connectors for power leads to disk drives. These are usually provided on clones because the power units are of a standard design, but if the supply has no connectors for drives you cannot proceed unless you buy a new power supply or add a set of drive cables to the existing one. In the absence of a circuit diagram and layout diagram for the power supply unit this would not be advisable. If you are familiar with the type of switch-mode supply that is used you can make up your own cables – always provide at least four drive connectors so as to provide for future expansion.

Now check the drive bays. You may need to loosen off the front panel to gain access to the lowest bay so that you can secure a drive to its sides – the bolt holes are usually inaccessible when the front panel is in place and the drive bays fastened down. Make sure that you have fastening bolts of the correct type for your drive(s). If the drive bay container is of the type that allows several 3.5″ drives to be mounted you are in luck, because this makes the installation of the hard drive much easier. If you have one 3.5″ bay and several 5.25″ bays you can install new drives using adapter plates.

You will not normally be using a 5.25″ hard drive unless you have obtained a large-capacity units of this size, such as the Quantum Bigfoot, at a bargain price. If the computer already uses large hard drives these will often be intended for use with a SCSI connection rather than an IDE one. SCSI connections on PC machines are not so thoroughly standardized (or so common) as the IDE type, so you are on your own unless you can obtain manuals for the drive and its interface card.

Always install the hard drive first, in the lowest bay or in a sideways position if this is available. If no sideways fasteners are provided, you will need to bolt the drive into the lowest bay and then bolt the set of bays into the case – after checking that the drive is firmly in place. Replace the front panel if you have had to remove it. Connect the power cable connector to the power connector on the drive, making sure that the two are correctly engaged. The point about using the lowest bay is that this one has a permanent front cover – the bays above will have removable front covers so that floppy drives can be installed.

If you need also to install a floppy drive, do so now, or replace whatever floppy drive was on the machine if it lacked only the hard drive. Remember that a 3.5″ drive will often require an adapter for its power supply, and these are not always easy to find in local shops. If the machine has come with a 3.5″ floppy drive included, check that this is not a 720 Kbyte drive – you will need the 1.4 Mbyte variety for most software packages. The cost of a floppy drive of either type is under £30 at the time of writing.

As a small note, the main difference between a 3.5″ 1.4 Mbyte floppy and a 3.5″ 720 Kbyte floppy is the second hole in the casing. Some modern drives allow you to treat a 720 Kbyte disk as if it were a 1.4 Mbyte type, ignoring the absence of the hole; older drives in general will use the presence of the hole to indicate a high density disk. This hole need not be square, and a hole of around 3/8″ diameter in the right place will work wonders, Figure 7.1. You must, of course, format each drilled disk afterwards. Of some 200 720 Kbyte disks I have drilled in this way, only one refused to format as a 1.4 Mbyte disk – and that was a disk given away with a magazine. If you have a large number of 720 Kbyte floppies, 15 minutes with your Black and Decker is time well spent – but make sure that all the dust and swarf is totally removed before you format and use the disks.

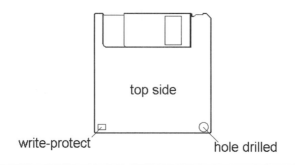

top side

write-protect

hole drilled

7.1 How to convert an old 720 Kbyte floppy to format at 1.4 Mbyte.

At the upgrading stage, you might want to consider drives other than straightforward magnetic drives. The options currently are floptical disks, tape streamers, and read/write optical drives. These latter drives are still fairly expensive, and unless you were able to find one on offer they are not currently a popular item for building in to a DIY machine. Floptical drives are conventional magnetic drives which use a laser guidance system to write much narrower and close-packed tracks. This allows a 3.5″ disk to hold some 100 Mbyte, a useful size for backing up files. The drives are not cheap compared to conventional 3.5″ types, though, and the disks are expensive. For backup purposes (meaning that you will not necessarily need to read the files back very often), a tape streamer can be much more cost effective.

Currently, conventional tape streamers, other than the DAT type, of 500 Mbyte (upwards) sizes are inexpensive, and the tape cartridges that they use are also inexpensive. If you need the peace of mind that backups provide (or you feel that your bargain hard drive might not be such a bargain for long) then a streamer of this type can be a good buy. It is installed in much the same way as a conventional 5.25″ floppy drive. Avoid parallel port devices unless you have no bays available – remember that you will probably need to install an additional parallel port for such a device.

Remember that when you have made changes to floppy or hard drives you will have to notify these changes to the CMOS RAM of the machine as detailed in Chapter 6. Some tape streamers make use of the floppy data cable, and do not need to be notified in the CMOS RAM.

Graphics card

If you are upgrading, the need to upgrade the graphics card is less immediate than the need to upgrade disk drives, because the VGA type of card has been a standard for some considerable time. Machines that used a CGA card are likely to be thoroughly obsolete by now, and not worth the trouble and expense of upgrading. You might, however, want to upgrade the graphics card so as to speed up the use of Windows or to be able to use the higher SVGA modes such as 800×600 graphics in 256 or more colours.

Your choice of graphics card is important if you want to perform such an upgrade. If you are retaining an existing motherboard your choice is limited to the slower cards because only ISA slots will be available. If you are also upgrading a motherboard and going for a Socket-7 type, the new motherboard will use some PCI local bus slots, which operate at a much higher speed than the ordinary slots. If you want to take advantage of this extra speed, you will need to buy a graphics card that is designed for use with a PCI bus. You can expect to pay up to £150 for such a graphics card, though the lower cost cards are very effective, and faster than almost any card on a conventional bus. This applies also to some of the ultra-fast cards that use the ordinary bus structure and which can be used on older machines. If you want ultra-fast 3-D graphics and video, you will have to pay more, use an AGP slot, and ensure that the rest of your computer is as fast as it can be made.

Ports

If you need more than the standard allocation, upgrading ports is simple enough in mechanical terms by inserting a card, but you need to give thought to setting jumpers or DIP switches before doing this. The main problem is that you probably have one parallel port and two serial ports on the motherboard or on a separate existing IDE card. This means that any port card you add is likely to cause some conflict with the existing ports unless you are careful to select the correct address and interrupt settings. Chapter 5 contains details of what to look for. One important reason for upgrading ports is likely to be the use of a modem, and since this is a topic that requires some thought and a lot of information, see Chapter 10.

Updating the motherboard

The complete upgrading of an old computer using a new motherboard involves stripping the PC down to an empty case. The old motherboard has its earthing bolts removed, and spring clips held closed, and eased out. You can then install another motherboard in the way described in Chapter 2. Less drastic steps are upgrading memory, video card and hard drive(s). Do not be tempted by offers of upgrading a processor chip, usually by way of an accelerator board which replaces the old chip, because this is often more costly than upgrading the motherboard, and leaves you with a motherboard whose performance may not be up to that of the chip. Upgrading a chip is an option only if you have a motherboard using Socket-7 which can be set to take a faster chip. For example, if you have a motherboard with a 166MMX Pentium, you can easily upgrade to 233MMX Pentium (possibly to 266MMX or higher if the board can cope) by fitting a new processor.

- You cannot upgrade a Socket-7 motherboard with a Pentium-II chip because the Pentium-II chips use a different form of holder, Slot-1, which resembles a SIMM holder. At the moment, several new machines use Pentium-II (because of price cuts by Intel on chips supplied to manufacturers) but it is likely that fast chips for Socket-7 boards will be offered for some considerable time by other suppliers. For example, at the time of writing, AMD has announced a 300 MHz K6 processor, but you would have to be sure that this could be fitted into your motherboard, because older motherboards will not accept a chip running at more than 233 MHz. The use of a Pentium-II board will not necessarily provide a speed advantage unless your software can make use of the special features of the chip, and there are very few items of software that you are likely to use that can take advantage of the very expensive dual-Pentium type of motherboard. Note that the cut-down version of Pentium-II is now called Celerix.

The memory of a modern machine will be held in SIMM form, and for practical purposes we need only consider the 72-pin EDO SIMM type. A typical motherboard will have four EDO SIMM holders, allowing it to take up to 128 Mbyte of memory, but you should not use more than 64 Mbyte unless you are certain that your software will cope with the extra. Most modern motherboards will provide DIMM sockets (with restrictions on mixing DIMM and SIMM use), and some offer six SIMM sockets rather than the conventional four.

You should *not* add memory to an existing motherboard unless you have the documentation for the motherboard, which is not always easy to achieve when you are refurbishing a machine. Old motherboards were constructed so that jumpers or switches had to be set before adding memory, and incorrect settings could cause damage to the memory chips. More modern motherboards are de-signed so that, provided the memory is added in the correct way, no jumper or switch settings are needed.

One thing that both older and more recent motherboards have in common is that memory is arranged in banks. This is done so as to make it impossible for the same part of memory to be addressed twice in rapid succession, and each bank is used alternately, giving the memory in a bank time to settle before it is used again. This allows slower memory chips to be used in each bank without com-promising the speed of the processor. The point about using banked memory is that you cannot use odd amounts of memory because SIMMs must be installed in pairs.

Memory and program problems

Programs (or *applications*, as they are often called) are the main source of trouble for the PC user. The programs need not be trouble-some in themselves, but the way that they use memory, interact with other programs and require response from the user all add up to potential trouble, particularly for the user who believes that reading manuals or books would be a waste of time. This section, then, is devoted to the memory problems that can arise simply from the use of modern programs in upgraded machines (new wine in old bottles?), and we need to start with some basic ideas and recollections about programs and memory.

The main (RAM) memory of a computer behaves like a set of switches, each of which can be set to be on or off, and each remaining as it is set only for the time during which power is applied to the computer. A set of eight of these switch-like units is called one byte of memory. This size of memory unit is important, because this is the unit into which memory is organized, even if the computer works with larger units of two (16-bit) or four (32-bit) bytes at a time. One byte of memory is sufficient to store any character that can be represented in ASCII code, and memory sizes are always measured in units of kilobytes (1024 bytes) or megabytes (1 048 576 bytes). The use of the prefixes kilo and mega in this way is peculiar to computing, normally kilo means 1000 and mega means 1 000 000, and the reason for the difference is that the memory 'switches' can be set one of two ways, so that numbers have to be stored in twos. 1024 is 2 to the power 10, so that this is preferred to the use of 1000 for computing purposes.

The microprocessor of the computer can gain access to any byte of memory by a very simple system of numbering each byte and using the number, called the address number, as a reference. In order to gain access to memory, the microprocessor must place signals corresponding to the address number on to a set of lines called the address bus, and there must be memory physically present which responds that the address. It's all very simple and logical so far, but this is where the problems start. The original 8088/8086 processors that were used on the original IBM PC machines (and the many clones that were constructed later) were capable of addressing 1 Mbyte (1024 Kbyte) of memory, an amount which at the time was thought to be ridiculously excessive. This does not mean, however, that all of this 1 Mbyte of memory can be RAM that can be used by programs. The machine needs some memory to be present in permanent (ROM) form, and some address numbers need to be reserved for this section of the memory. The microprocessor chip is made so that when it is first switched on or reset, it will try to read memory at a specific address, number 1 048 560. This is built into the chip and cannot be altered, so that any computer using the Intel chips must provide for the BIOS program to start at this address – the remainder of the routines can be elsewhere as long as the start is at this fixed address.

A further complication is added by the use of the graphics card. The video signal depends on using memory, and the PC type of machine reserves memory addresses for this purpose, the video memory, with the RAM chips for this placed on the video graphics card itself. The amount that is needed depends on the type of video card that is being used, with SVGA requiring 2 Mbyte or more, EGA and VGA requiring a minimum of 256. Finally, the MS-DOS operating system, certainly in versions prior to 4.0, can use only 640 Kbyte of RAM for programs.

The Pentium class of machine uses a processor which can address very much more memory than the chips used in the original PC and XT machines, and the usual limit is 128 Mbyte, though some motherboards cater for more than this. This makes no difference as far as running MS-DOS programs is concerned, because they cannot use more than 640 Kbyte of memory, but Windows can make full use of memory up to 64 Mbyte.

Your installed programs add another dimension to all this. When a program is installed in the approved way, it leaves entries into a database inside Windows called the Registry. If these entries are incorrect you can expect problems with some programs, notably Windows itself and all of the Microsoft Office set, though some older programs will run perfectly without problems because they use older methods. This is why you can encounter so many difficulties if you try to transfer all your programs from one hard drive to another. There are programs, such as DriveCopy and Drive Image, that make this task easier by ensuring that Registry entries and links between programs are correctly made on the new copy.

Chapter 8

Multimedia and other connections

CD-ROM

CD-ROM is by now an essential part of a computer because so much software is now distributed in this form. The use of CD-ROM is obligatory if you want to make use of multimedia programs, in which text, sound and graphics are all featured. The amount of data that is involved in some modern programs, and in items such as graphics files, makes the use of conventional magnetic disks inadequate – a set of 100 3.5″ disks is a major expense in media let alone in contents.

The alternative is to use a CD, since the CD system was intended from the start to be a way of coding and storing digital signals. The original CD-ROM drives operated at the same speed as the conventional audio CD players, but this is much too slow for computing purposes, and drives are rated by their speed relative to the audio type. A reasonably fast speed for modern purposes is 16×, meaning that the drive can spin the disc 16 times faster than an audio CD player, and speeds of 24× and 32× can also be obtained.

Compact discs are the same size as the old 5.25″ magnetic disks, but use laser-light technology to store data. Because a laser light beam can be focused with a high degree of precision, the tracks on these discs can be much closer together than is the case with magnetic disks. As a result, they have very high capacities, measured in hundreds of Mbytes (typically, 600 Mbytes). The same technology used for recording and playing music CDs is used for computer compact discs. Another advantage is the fact that data are more secure on compact discs, as they cannot be corrupted by magnetic fields. The discs are referred to as CD-ROM, using the title ROM as a reminder that you cannot write on such discs, only read them.

CD-ROM discs have a large data capacity (around 650 Mbyte for a standard 5″ disc) and high packing density. The devices are available in one of two forms. The permanent Write Once, Read Many or WORM disc is effectively a read-only memory using the format of an audio CD, and the more recent erasable and re-recordable types are at the time of writing much more expensive, both for the drive and for the blank disc.

Discs consist of a glass or (more usually) plastic platter that carries a very thin, sensitive, vacuum-deposited layer on one side, to act as the memory. This layer is then coated with a transparent layer for protection and two such disks can be glued back to back to form a double-sided memory. Data are encoded on an optical disc by burning tiny pits in its surface with laser light. A pit represents a binary 1, the absence of a pit represents 0. Laser light is also used to read data from the disc, the pits and non-pits setting up different light-inference patterns that can be detected by the reading head. Retrieval times are faster than floppy drives, though not as fast as hard drive systems. Early CD-ROM players were referred to as single speed, meaning that the speed of data recovery was much the same as that of an audio CD. Since then, faster drives have been manufactured, and names such as 4 speed, 6 speed, 12 speed, 24 speed and higher have been used to refer to the speed relative to the older standard. Very fast drives are better able to cope with the need for fast-changing data, such as video.

Several types of compact disc systems are available for computers. These are:

- CD-ROM. Like music CDs, these are 'pressed' by the manufacturers with whatever data they wish to supply. Large databases of information can be supplied in this way, as can software. This form is economical only if large numbers are being pressed.

- WORM. The Write Once, Read Many type of drive allows you to write a disc with your data, and this data can be read as many times as required. Once written, this type of disc cannot be written again. WORM drives are useful for creating archive backups. This type of drive is now called CD-R.
- Erasable optical discs. These use magneto-optical (MO) technology, and like ordinary magnetic disks allow you to record and erase data as often as you like. Unlike ordinary optical discs, the active layer of these discs is magnetized. To write a binary 1 to a spot on this layer, a pulse of laser light is focused on it, heating it up to several hundred degrees. At this temperature its magnetic polarity can be altered by a magnet which is activated on the opposite side of the disc, but the remaining cold spots are unaffected by this magnet. Erasable optical drives are now available at prices of around £300, and, like all prices of computing equipment, this level is more likely to go down than up. This type of drive is now called CD-RW.

The general principle of reading a disc is indicated in Figure 8.1. About 10 mW of laser light energy is focused on to the sensitive surface to write the data. The exact effect depends upon the technology used. Reading is accomplished by using the same laser but at a

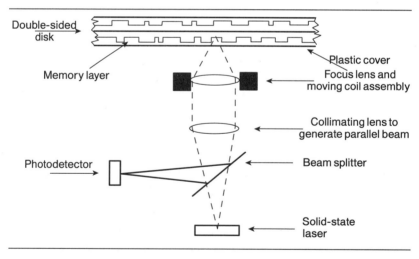

8.1 The use of a laser beam to read the pattern of dots on a CD type of disc. This is a generalized diagram, and takes no account of differences in drives.

much reduced power level of typically 0.5 mW. The reflected light energy is split from the main laser beam and focused on to a photodetector to regenerate the data. To ensure correct focus, a final lens in mounted in a moving coil assembly that is driven by part of the servo system. The drive signals for this and other positional control being obtained from the recovered data signal path.

Disks are available in several sizes ranging up to 5″ for computer use. The 5″ version is described as a *CD-ROM* because the concept is closely related to that of the compact audio disk, and the storage size is around 650 Mbytes. The standard speed CD-ROM drive provides an output bit rate of 125 kbit/s, but a modern 24-speed drive will read at a rate of 3 Mbits per second.

READ/WRITE SYSTEMS

Dye polymer technology. Certain organic dyes, including alloys of zinc and silver can be used as a coating for a writeable disc. When a very thin layer of the material is exposed to laser light, local heating causes microscopic pits or craters to be formed to provide a permanent memory. The amount of light that can be reflected from the surface now varies according to the pit pattern. The reflected light energy has a different and varying phase from the incident beam and so it can be extracted as the data signal. Other organic dyes will change colour when exposed to a laser beam, because the laser beam causes local spots to change between different crystalline states. The colour changes again vary the reflectance. This dye-colour method can be used to produce erasable and reusable discs.

Heat sensitive technology. In this type of disc, the sensitive layer is an alloy of tellurium and selenium with a light doping of arsenic to give more accurate control of the melting point. When the disc is being written, the laser beam burns microscopic holes in the sensitive layer and these are detected by the lower power beam during a read action. The disc can be erased by using just enough laser energy to melt the layer without forming holes. The molten regions then cool very quickly to solidify into a stable amorphous state. Rewriting ensures final erasure by transforming the amorphous domains back into the crystalline state.

Magneto-optical technology (M-O). This system is also called optically assisted magnetic recording. A thin layer of amorphous gadolinium–iron–cobalt is used for the memory and the whole surface is initially magnetically polarized in the same plane but at right angles to the surface. When heat from a laser beam is applied simultaneously with a magnetic field from the other side of the disk, this small region reverses polarity and becomes frozen in this state. When plane polarized light is reflected from a highly polished electromagnetic surface, the light becomes elliptically polarized. This is the Kerr Effect. A read operation is therefore performed using polarized laser light to detect the field changes. For erasure, the surface is again laser heated but with the applied magnetic field polarized as in the original sense.

CD-ROM DRIVES

The form of CD-ROM drives is fairly well standardized now, as a slim 5.25″ casing. When a button on the front panel is pressed, a tray slides out so that a CD can be placed in the tray, and pressing the button again will cause the tray to slide back in. The drive motor then spins the disc (taking a second or so to build up to full speed), and from then on the disc can be accessed, usually as drive D:, or it will run its program(s) automatically. The front panel, Figure 8.2, reveals a drive-on light, a volume control and a headphone jack. This allows the use of the drive for playing ordinary

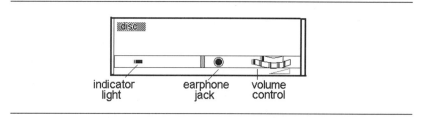

8.2 A typical CD-ROM drive front panel.

audio compact discs (or you could listen to your data). The output audio signal is typically 0.6 V r.m.s. at 1 kHz.

The CD-ROM drive uses three connectors, the power connector feeding +5 V and +12 V DC, an audio connector for amplifiers, and the data interface. The audio interface typically uses a 4-pin connector with connections:

1	Right channel	2	Earth
3	Left channel	4	Earth

and the data interface uses a 40-pin insulation displacement connector. On this connector, all the even-numbered pins from 4 onwards are earth connections, and the other pins are connected as follows:

1	Address bit 0 input	2	Address bit 1 input
5,7,9,11	Not connected	13	Interrupt output
15	Data request output	17	Data acknowledgement input
19	Read enable input	21	Write enable input
23	Bus enable input	25	Data bit 0
27	Data bit 1	29	Data bit 2
31	Data bit 3	33	Data bit 4
35	Data bit 5	37	Data bit 6
39	Data bit 7		

The CD-ROM is also the basis of multimedia work. Multimedia means that a CD can contain program code, digitized images and digital sound, and all of these can be used by the computer if a suitable sound system board is also added. This allows you to use encyclopaedia CDs that display text, images and can also play sound. For anyone whose interests include music the use of multimedia promises effects that are unmatched by any other medium, even video tape, because of the extent of the control that the computer program exerts over the display. For multimedia work it is desirable to have a fast (16× or more) CD-ROM drive, because the older low-speed units are handicapped when rapidly changing pictures have to be displayed.

- Installation of a CD-ROM drive has to be carried out early in the order of commissioning a new machine or one using a new motherboard and hard drive, because Windows will normally be installed from the CD-ROM drive. The drive package should include a floppy that will get the drive working from MS-DOS so that you can install Windows. You might find, however, that the program MSCDEX.EXE is missing, and that the CD-ROM drive cannot be installed until this program is present on the floppy. The MSCDEX.EXE file should be on the Startup floppy or on your MS-DOS floppies if you have them.

When you have the hard drive formatted with the MS-DOS system tracks, the next step is to install the driver for the CD-ROM from its floppy. Once this is done, you can boot the computer so that you see the MS-DOS prompt C:> and you can type D: to change this to D:>, meaning that the CD-ROM drive is detected and logged on. You can now insert a CD into the drive, such as the Windows CD, and run the Setup program on the CD. Note that the Windows CD will autorun only if you are using it on a machine that already has Windows (an earlier version, for example) installed.

CD-R AND CD-RW

The fast CD-ROM drives are read-only, but recently both write-once and write-repeatedly drives have been developed. The write-once type are known as CD-R, meaning CD recordable, and the write-often types as CD-RW (CD rewriters). These drives use the same size and style of casing, but their read speeds are much slower, typically 4× to 6×, with slower writing speeds. The write-once CD-R drives can use blank discs that are very attractively priced (at around £1) and which like the standard CD will hold about 650 Mbyte of data. Compression can increase this to around 1 Gbyte. The CD-RW drives cost more, and the blank discs current retail at around £17. You can expect this price to drop, and unless you are absolutely certain that you would never want to use the RW type, you can hedge your bets with a drive that can use both types of discs. Currently, a CD-R drive cannot read the discs made by the CD-RW type, and vice versa, so that the all-in-one drive is well worth any extra expense.

The design and availability of these drives changes rapidly, so check out what is available in magazines such as *Computer Shopper* before you make any decisions, and look out for improvements in speed and reductions in price. You may feel that you want to hang on to your present fast CD reader, but some CD-RW drives cannot share a connection, so that you might not be able to run both together. Drives that can use both types of discs will show three sets of speeds, such as 2× 2× 6×, meaning that the write-once speed is 2×, the write-again speed is 2× and the read speed is 6×.

DVD

DVD (Digital Video Disc) is an alternative to CD-ROM. DVD means digital versatile disc, a development of CD that can store much larger amounts of data and transfer them more rapidly. The versatility that forms part of the name arises because the DVD can be used for computer data, music or video. A DVD can be single sided, single layer, storing 4.7 Gbyte as compared to the 650 Mbyte of CD, and the double-sided two-layer version of DVD can store 17 Gbyte. Like CDs, DVD can be obtained as read-only, write-once (DVD-R), or DVD-RAM (read/write).

Windows 98 supports the use of several makes of DVD drives. This allows you to use video playback of discs to your TV receiver if you have the DVD decoder card and suitable software for a PAL type of TV display.

Sound boards

The most common reason for wanting to add a sound board to a PC is so as to be able to use multimedia fully. This is particularly important if your interests are in music or other sound-related topics. The other common requirement that is more biased to business is to be able to input sound, such as using a voice dictation program like the IBM *Via Voice*, or placing a spoken commentary with an image or a document. The software for such commentary requirements is built into Windows, but the hardware has to be added. Multimedia packages usually consist of CD-ROM player with sound card, loudspeakers, microphone and a range of software.

- Note that if you buy a voice dictation package you should use the microphone that came with the package rather than any other you have obtained with a sound card. Microphone sensitivity and positioning are the factors that take most time to get used to when you start to use a dictation package.

The Windows software includes a number of files which use the WAV extension, and which will provide sound outputs such as chimes and ringing notes. These can be set so that they are associated with events such as incoming messages, errors, disk saving and so on, acting as a reminder of what you are doing. You either like this or loathe it, and it is up to you whether you activate it or not. By contrast, the Sound Recorder software in Windows allows you to input sound from a microphone or a cassette recorder and record it as a WAV file. You can then embed this into a document (for example) in the form of a visible icon. When you are reading the document, clicking on the icon will play back the sound recording. There are also sound editor facilities (echo, mix, blend, play faster or slower) built into Windows.

The Media Player software of Windows allows devices such as audio CDs or video discs to be controlled by the computer, and a standard form of musical instrument digital interface (MIDI) allows the computer to be used to control electronic instruments such as synthesizers. One point to remember, however, is that digital sound requires large amounts of storage space on a disk – one often-quoted example is that one minute of speech can require more than 600 Kbyte of disk space. This requirement can be reduced by using data-compression techniques built into the software, but you need to be aware of how much disk space is likely to be used. Even more space is needed for the AVI type of compressed video files.

A typical sound-board package will consist of the card itself, two active loudspeakers (not always of high quality) and a microphone, probably with a MIDI interface built into the board, and additional software that can be used to replace or supplement the software supplied in Windows. The board is plugged into a slot (usually an ISA slot) in the usual way, and the other units are connected to it.

- An active loudspeaker set has amplifiers built into one of the loudspeaker boxes and draws power from the mains, rather than from the computer. It requires an audio connection to the loudspeaker

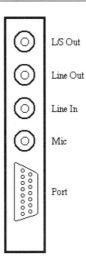

8.3 Typical sound card connections. Apart from the game port, these are made using 3.5 mm stereo jack plugs.

output of the sound card and a mains connection. An earphone can be operated from the line-out terminal of the card.

In selecting an add-on sound system, you should consider the quality of sound from the loudspeakers before anything else, because you may find it difficult to live with poor-quality sound. The lower cost packages are likely to omit a microphone, and, more important, will omit software that allows sound files to be compressed so as to take up less disk space. The software is the next important item, and should be suitable for your requirements. One standard item should allow you to add narration to documents or images, and another piece of software that is often included is a voice synthesizer which will read text from a spreadsheet or a word processed document (usually contained in the Windows clipboard). This latter application can often be, on its own, justification for adding a sound board. Some boards come only with software suitable for games. Figure 8.3 illustrates typical sound card output/input connections.

- At one time, the comparatively slow data transfer speeds for sound cards meant that only the ISA card connection could be used. Some modern cards, notably the Pine Schubert series, can be obtained with PCI connectors, and this can be very useful if you have only a few ISA slots, one of which is already occupied with a modem and another with a SCSI card.

The game port on a sound card uses a 15-pin D-type socket, whose connections are as follows:

Pin 1	+5 V	Pin 2	Paddle 1 button, joystick A
Pin 3	Paddle 1 position, joystick A *x*-co-ordinate	Pin 4	Earth
Pin 5	Earth	Pin 6	Paddle 2 position, joystick A *y*-co-ordinate
Pin 7	Paddle 2 button	Pin 8	Earth
Pin 9	Earth	Pin 10	Paddle 3 button, joystick B button
Pin 11	Paddle 3 position, joystick B *x*-co-ordinate	Pin 12	Earth
Pin 13	Paddle 4 position, joystick B *y*-coordinate	Pin 14	Paddle 4 button
Pin 15	+5 V		

Scanners, digital cameras and graphics pads

A scanner is a useful method of obtaining a graphics file from a picture, so that you can edit, select and transform the picture to your own needs. Scanners come as low-cost hand scanners, medium-price roller scanners, or higher cost A4 flat-bed types, and unless your needs are very limited you should not consider the hand type. If you need to do a lot of detailed work on printed images, some of which are more than 4″ wide, or you need to scan text into image form and then convert this to text form, only the roller or the flat-bed type of page scanner will suffice. These are now very reasonably priced in the £100 to £200 range. You will have to decide for yourself if you need high-resolution colour or if your needs can be served by black and white images—most scanners will provide both, and you cannot now expect to find a scanner that costs less because it provides for monochrome only. These scanners usually come packaged with OCR (Optical Character Recognition) software that will convert the image of words (which is just a pattern of dots) into computer text (using one code for each character). The better types of OCR can be used on existing picture files or text, not simply those that have been scanned recently.

Fitting a scanner involves using either the parallel port or the use of a SCSI interface card, and you may need to set jumpers on this card in accordance with the manufacturer's instructions. SCSI cards that are supplied along with scanners are often of a simplified design, and cannot necessarily be used to interface other SCSI devices. You need to plan carefully if you want to install both a SCSI scanner and another SCSI device, because you may need to buy a separate (and expensive) SCSI interface card that will supply both.

All scanners require fairly elaborate software. At its simplest, the software will be of the bit-mapped graphics variety, so that the scanned image is converted into a file. This is usually of the 'standard' TIFF (Tag Image File Format) – the trouble is that different manufacturers have their own ideas about TIFF standards so that software that reads TIFF files might not read *your* TIFF file. Another consideration is time and memory, because it can take several minutes or so for a flat-bed scanner to read an elaborate A4 page, and at full resolution it might need some 150 Mbyte or more of disk space to store the file.

- All scanners quote two resolution figures. The lower is the *optical* resolution, meaning the genuine image resolution that the scanner can detect. The higher figure is the interpolated resolution, which is obtained by using software to fill in additional dots between the ones that are supplied from the scanner. The interpolation action can provide very high-resolution figures, around 9500 dots per inch or more, and the corresponding files are very large.

The first question you need to ask yourself is whether you need such a device. If you are working with DTP and need an occasional graphic, the extensive libraries of clip art will probably hold enough to keep you in images for the foreseeable future, even if you sometimes need to have an image converted for special purposes. The second point is the type of image you want to read. If this is a simple black-and-white logo or pattern, then it is quite likely that a low-cost scanner could provide as much as you need, particularly if you can retouch the image later by any type of drawing program. If on the other hand you need to be able to read photographs or drawings that contain a large range of grey shades, or work with elaborate OCR then you will certainly require a much more elaborate roller or flat-bed scanner, with matching software.

- For some purposes you might want to invest in one of the all-in-one devices that combine a scanner with an inkjet printer to make a scanner, copier and printer unit.
- At the time of writing, the prices of scanners and their associated software have dropped very rapidly, and you can now get a flat-bed scanner at a price that would once have been considered reasonable for a hand-held type.

You almost always have to choose between line art (black-and-white drawings) and photographs. For reproducing line art you want the high resolution with no grey-scale capabilities. For photographs you need comparatively low resolution, but probably 24-bit or higher colour (photo-real colour). Scanners can usually be switched (by software) to fulfil either of these requirements really well.

CAMERAS

A more recent type of image grabber uses a camcorder as the scanning device, because the camcorder is such a familiar consumer item that many computer users possess one. The problem is that all but the most upmarket digital camcorders have poor resolution figures so that images taken from them are not of high quality. The same applied to images taken directly from TV broadcasts or from videos, though you will see many such images on the Internet. Copying images from TV or video also raises problems of copyright. Image grabbing requires both added hardware to connect the PC to the camera, TV or video, and software to carry out the grabbing action.

More recently, attention has switched to digital still cameras. These use low-resolution sensors and store the digitized image on memory cards (a few on disks) so that the image files can be transferred to the computer by a simple interface. The lower cost digital cameras are suitable only for simple illustrations, and some have very low resolution (320×240), but the 640×480 types can produce acceptable pictures, given a good colour printer. No digital camera at the time of writing provides a picture of photographic quality, and no printer is really up to that standard either, but you should judge for yourself what is acceptable to you. After all, we spend much of our time watching TV pictures that are certainly not of photographic standard, and it is probably unfair to judge by the high standards of the local camera club. Remember that better image quality also means very large image files, and the need to print images on very expensive paper. If you want to make images of newspaper standard then the 640×480 standard of camera is adequate, but at present these are very primitive compared to film cameras. Do not expect zoom lenses, auto-focus or any of the features that we take for granted in film cameras of quite reasonable price ranges.

Another source of images is now the digital type of camcorder, particularly those that allow a still image to be recorded. Several of these feature a Firewire type of output connection, and some allow both reading and writing of the tape, allowing images to be edited and replaced on the tape. This is not a useful option unless your computer possesses a Firewire port, with software for reading, editing and writing.

GRAPHICS TABLETS

Another option for images is the use of graphics tablets or digitizers, which require an interface board. The graphics tablet looks like a small drawing board with a stylus, and its action is to control the cursor. The action is not like that of a mouse, because each position on the graphics board corresponds exactly to a position on the screen, allowing you to trace drawings, for example. Pressing the stylus corresponds to clicking the left-hand mouse button, and the driver software allows for a key combination to carry out the action of the right-hand mouse button. You can use this to create drawings either directly or by tracing an existing image, and at the current price of equipment this can often be a cheaper option than a scanner.

Most graphics tablets allow you to control a CAD directly from the tablet, and most will allow tracing of photographs or drawings. Do not, however, rush into buying a tablet, even at an attractive price, unless you are sure that it has a good Windows 98 driver. Another point to watch is the size of the tablets, because the prices are often quoted for the A6 size, which is 105 mm × 148 mm, about $4\frac{1}{4}'' \times 5\frac{3}{4}''$. If you are concerned with small illustrations, this may be adequate, but for your purposes it might be too small, and the price of graphics tablets is proportional to their area, making A4 tablets very expensive.

TELETEXT AND VIDEO CARDS

Teletext and TV cards are intended to take the signals from a TV aerial and extract the picture signals and the teletext information from the normal BBC and ITV transmissions (*not* from satellite transmissions). These provide a wide range of information from the Ceefax and Oracle services, and because there is no form of charging for the information, unlike Internet information, you can browse over the data, saving to disk as you choose. You can also print out the information, a very valuable feature if you want to retain data that will not be repeated, such as the recipes in a cookery program, or the week's Radio and TV program schedules.

● One of the curious omissions on TV receivers, at a time when any sort of gimmick is used to make one brand stand out from others, is that there is no way of connecting a printer to print out the Teletext pages. At one time this would have been impossible because older receivers were connected directly to the mains with no earth, but for some considerable time now TV receivers have used earthed frames and the Teletext portion uses digital chips.

The Teletext data option has been one that has been strangely neglected by users, to such an extent that the Teletext cards can be quite difficult to find. This is due to some extent to the unique nature of Teletext – there is no corresponding service in the USA. Look for Teletext cards from ATi and Hauppauge, the main UK sources for such cards. If you can connect the Teletext card to a good signal source from an aerial this form of data access is very much more useful than the Internet for a lot of the UK-specific information that is available, and without the cost and restriction of telephone lines.

Networks

Networking means connecting computers together so that they can share resources such as printers and hard disks. This allows any user of a machine in the network to print to the one laser printer in the system without such expedients as placing the file on a disk to load into the machine that is connected to the printer. It allows users of a database to update files, knowing that these same files are available in updated form to each user. It allows a document to be seen on each screen in the network if it is important to have everyone's attention drawn to it. For a number of users, networking promises a considerably easier life than the use of separate machines.

The promise is not always easily fulfilled. Successful networking requires a mixture of hardware and software that must be adequate for the purpose, well installed and explained thoroughly to all users. Few experienced users of networks who now feel confident in their use would care to go through the initial stages of networking all over again. Imperfection in networking can mean losing files, programs running slowly, endless error messages on programs that have been previously totally reliable.

The problems are notoriously difficult to locate, and the blame for problems is shifted around faster than a hot potato. Such problems do not necessarily point to a network system being a bad one, because there are so many factors involved in a network as compared to the simplicity of a one-user, one-machine set of systems. Network manuals are not famed for being written in clear English or for dealing with the problems that users so often experience. Networking may in some cases not even be appropriate, and users could obtain all that they want by passing disks around and by the use of a printer switch.

Fortunately, many of the problems that attended the pioneers of networking have now disappeared. Windows 95 and Windows 98 are very much more suited to networking than the older versions ever were, and the software writers are more experienced in coping with network use. The extent of the problems can be gauged by thinking about a few simple examples. What happens, for instance, if two network users require the printer at the same time or want to alter the same data file at the same time? Suppose that some files are to be allowed to be used by only a few users and hidden from others? How does one user place a message on the screen of another user or use a Windows program that is located in another computer?

All networking systems require additional software to cope with these tasks of allocation and priority that MS-DOS was never intended to solve. In addition, there is the hardware task of wiring up machines to each other, because there are several methods of connecting machines, and a networking card will have to be present (except for some very simple systems like Interlink or Direct Cable Connection) in each machine that is connected. A really extensive network can be very costly and require at least one machine, the server, that is quite exceptionally fast. In this sense, a server is a computer which is directly connected to a resource such as a hard disk (the file server) or a printer (the printer server), and it is quite common for this machine to be connected to all the important resources.

A server can be dedicated or non-dedicated. A dedicated server does nothing else other than supply the other machines; a non-dedicated server is used like any other machine in the network with an operator keying in data and looking at the screen. If this operator should absent-mindedly switch off, the whole network goes down. The non-dedicated server will need more software in memory than the dedicated type, so that it may not be able to run large programs, and is likely to run slowly. A dedicated server can make use of all its memory for a network operating system and does not necessarily need to use MS-DOS at all. For a network of more than three users, this is almost always a better approach. Another form of non-dedicated server is the peer-to-peer network in which each computer contains enough networking software to act either as a server or a receiver, and no machine is tied up because another one is using its files.

The smallest and simplest networks make use, for connections, of the serial ports on each computer, limiting them to the maximum rate of data transfer of a serial port and requiring no extra cards (unless there are other demands for the serial port). This type of system can be used for printer sharing and for limited file transfer, but is not up to the task of, for example, allowing a database to be shared by several users. For the less-demanding applications, however, the use of the serial ports is an attractive low-cost option and it can make use of low-cost cables. Another option is to use the same software with parallel port connections, which makes the network much faster.

The next stage in complexity is a network in which each computer is fitted with an expansion card whose circuits provide for much faster transfer rates than can be obtained from serial or parallel ports (10 to 50 times faster typically). The connection is usually by four-core (twin-twisted) cable using connectors that are now standardized. Where the maximum cable length is less than a few hundred metres it would be pointless to use any more expensive cable system (such as data cable), and the software of the system is usually geared to the less-demanding uses.

The networks that are at the top of the range are all named varieties which are by now well known and well established, such as Ethernet, Token Ring and Novell. For large-scale users, the Novell network system is almost an automatic choice, particularly if the server is to be a mini rather than a micro computer.

In general, if you are considering networking a large number of computers with any of the major network systems, you will need either to be very experienced yourself or to take advice or have the work carried out by a qualified agent.

Direct Cable Connection (DCC)

DCC, which is part of the Windows package, is intended as a simple utility for connecting a laptop to a desktop computer, but it can also be used as an elementary form of network system for two desktop computers, using either parallel or serial ports. Most computers possess only one parallel port which is used for the printer, but it is quite common to fit two serial ports and even if one of these is used for a serial mouse this leaves one spare for DCC connection. If you need faster networking, you can fit additional parallel ports to each computer and buy a special cable.

- This type of simple interconnection does not rank as a network for the purposes of installing Windows.

Serial links, which are much more common for DCC, allow transfer rates of just over 115 000 bits per second, which is considerably slower than can be achieved with parallel ports, but fast enough for printing or file copying. The hardware consists simply of a seven-core serial non-modem cable terminated in the type of plugs that the machines use – either a 25-pin or a 9-pin type.

Serial cables that are intended for printers or external modems are useless – their connections are not suitable. You should specify that you want a *non-modem* (or *null-modem*) connected cable for linking two computers together. If parallel ports are to be used, the cable that is used to link the computers must be made or supplied specially – it is not a standard form of printer cable (it uses four data pins and four control pins on each connector, plus earth).

With DCC in use two machines can share drives and printers. One machine is designated as the *host* (server) and the other as the *guest* (client). When both machines are running DCC, the guest machine can make use of the files and (if this is set up) the printer(s) of the host. The host cannot use any facilities of the guest. Because the DCC programs run in their own windows, you can switch to a different window and use either machine for other purposes. You are not, however, allowed to alter a file that the other machine is using, and you can configure DCC so that files on the host are read-only as far as the guest is concerned. You can also decide whether or not to allow printer use by the guest machine.

- Note that if you did not install DCC when you installed Windows, you may find some difficulties in adding it. Using *Add/Remove Programs* from Control Panel will often result in a request to find files in the folder C:\Windows\MSDUN. You should ignore this and change the folder to, typically, D:\Win95 with the CD-ROM disc in the D: drive.
- DCC can be installed only if Dial-up Networking (DUN) is also installed, and when you select installation of DCC, Windows will ensure that DUN is also present.

You have to ensure that the Microsoft IPX/SPX protocols are being used by both computers. The *Help* action of DCC contains a

Troubleshooter that will allow you to check that everything is correctly set up. If this *Troubleshooter* does not sort out problems then the most likely reason is that you are using an incorrect cable, probably a serial cable that is not of the null-modem type or not fully connected. Another possibility is that the cable is connected to the wrong port (you may have specified COM1 when in fact you are using COM2).

You have to designate one computer as *Host* and the other as *Guest*. The *Guest* computer will be able to use the files and printer(s) of the *Host,* and you have to designate what folder(s) on the *Host* you want to share. The usual choice is the C:\ folder, and you can click on this with the right-hand mouse button and select Properties. In the Properties pane you click on *Sharing* and then fill in the details. You have to click the *Sharing As* button, and then fill in an identification for this folder (such as Host Hard Drive) that you will recognize on the other machine. You can also determine whether you want read-only sharing or full sharing, and whether you want to use passwording. When DCC is installed you will find a Sharing tab on the Printer properties pane, and this allows you to make sharing options for the printer as well.

Chapter 9

Windows

GUI methods

GUI (Graphics User Interface) is a term that has crept into computing language and which dates from the introduction of the Apple Macintosh. The unique feature of the Mac was (and still is) that the user does not type commands and press the ENTER key; instead commands are selected from a menu or a set of pictures (icons) by placing a cursor over the item, using a mouse, and clicking the mouse button. In addition, programs can be independently run within small screen areas, or windows, of their own. In theory, the user of a GUI machine need never type a command, and the Mac makes no provision for any form of type-and-press-ENTER commands other than in a 'dialogue box', a small form that the user fills in. The older name for GUI is WIMP, the initials of Windows, Icons, Mouse Programming.

The advantages of GUI methods are that once the basic principles are familiar it should be easier to learn to use any new program. In addition, it is never necessary to exercise your own memory too much. If you want to delete a file, for example, you will see a list of files in the selected folder and you can point to the one you want to erase and drag it to the picture of a waste bin (or press the Del key, which is much quicker). Contrast this with typing DEL and then the full path and file name (if you can remember it by then) for each file you want to delete. One of the reasons for the wholesale switch to GUI versions of established programs is to take advantage of easier learning. Other reasons are that the GUI itself contains screen and printer drivers, so that programs using the GUI do not need to supply their own drivers, and because so many programs can benefit from using a graphics screen display that is standardized by the GUI format.

On the other hand, GUI methods are often roundabout and for some actions a lot of mouse movement and clicking is needed. In addition, because a lot of the work of the processor is concerned simply with maintaining the pictorial display, there is less time to spend on the program you want to run. Some database programs do not exist in GUI versions because they would run at an unacceptably slow rate for actions such as searching for data. The PC type of machine allows you to make your own choice, with MS-DOS available for direct commands and for running a few programs (particularly games programs) at high speed, and the Windows GUI available for more leisurely work with the full range of windows, icons and mouse actions. Using Windows does not commit you exclusively to using the mouse for everything, because you can still use the keyboard for actions that are quicker done in that way – every user can devise his/her own best methods of working. Windows 98 offers speed improvements over earlier versions, particularly in its 'single-click' methods.

- Note that if you have no experience of using Windows you should read a suitable book, such as *Windows 95 Made Simple* or *Windows 98 Made Simple*. These books are written round the UK version of the GUI program concerned, rather than the US version which is described in the many high-priced books of US origin.

Windows has progressed through several versions, and the old Windows 3.1 version is still in use all over the world. If you are assembling a computer for use in the next few years, however, you are much more likely to want to use the most recent version of Windows which at the time of writing is Windows 98. If you are seeking to keep costs down, however, you might want to use a later (1997 onwards) version of its predecessor, Windows 95. The setting up of

Windows 95 is therefore described here, because it is essentially similar to the procedure of Windows 98.

- The later version of Windows 95, as supplied to manufacturers, allowed for the use of the FAT32 system (see page 47), but unless you bought a machine with this version in place you are not likely to have this version. Windows 98 is a development of this, allowing the FAT32 system to be installed even on a hard drive that already contains data, and the option for converting the hard drive to this system is a major difference between the installation of Windows 98 and Windows 95. You can install Windows 95/98 on a machine that already runs Windows 3.1, or on a machine that runs only the bare minimum of MS-DOS, whose hard drive has been formatted using the command: FORMAT C: /SYS. If you are installing on to a new hard drive, this latter method is the one that you will use.
- Windows 95/98 is a complete operating system in its own right, replacing both MS-DOS (partially) and Windows 3.1 (completely). Windows allows you to run both Windows and DOS programs, though a few DOS programs can be run only by baling out of Windows 95 completely.
- Note that Windows 98 is sold in two versions, the Upgrade version for anyone who already has Windows 3.1 or 95 installed, and the Full version for the user who is installing from scratch.

Windows 95/98 requires the use of a lot of memory, and the more memory your computer contains the better Windows 95 can use it. For most machines, adding extended memory means buying EDO SIMM modules. If you need to install additional memory, do so before you install Windows, on the old rule that you should never carry out two innovations at the same time. A memory size of 16 Mbyte is now regarded as a bare minimum, and performance is greatly enhanced by using 32 Mbyte or 64 Mbyte. Since Windows 95/98 is intended to be used on a modern type of machine it comes on a CD-ROM with a option for a set of 3.5″ 1.44 Mb disks. The use of the CD-ROM is illustrated in this book. The installation to a hard drive of adequate size is assumed – Windows 95/98 is simply not intended for machines with only floppy drives or with small (less than 500 Mbyte) hard drives. Even a moderate selection of Windows files will require about 80 Mbyte. The later Windows 95 version, and the Windows 98 version, contains Internet Explorer which adds to the space required on the hard drive. Note that disk directories are now called *folders*.

- The later version of Windows 95 included Internet Explorer, and this is true also of Windows 98. The built-in Web browser is excellent, but if you want to continuing a browser that you already have installed and you are familiar with there is nothing to stop you, and you can delete the Microsoft Internet Explorer files later if you wish.

SETUP

Because there are so many variations on the PC machine, using different video systems, keyboards, mice, and other features, and so many programs that can reside in the memory, it is impossible to test a new program such as Windows 95/98 with every available combination of machine and software. If you are using a straightforward 'clone' PC with straightforward business software (no games) it is likely that you will be able to run the Windows 95/98 Setup program and use Windows without problems.

- The README files on the CD-ROM are intended to notify you of problems that have arisen since Windows went into production, and you should check carefully for references to your machine or to software that might be running at the time when you install Windows. You can read these files with your existing word-processor software and print them *before* you start to install Windows. In particular, these files will warn you of known problems of incompatibility and their cure, if any.

PREPARING FOR INSTALLATION

The following description refers to a normal installation, meaning that your computer is not one that features in the README files, and you are not running any of the listed software that is known to cause problems. Fortunately, most of the awkward cases of hardware and software are not imported to the UK.

You can install Windows either from an earlier version (meaning Windows 3.1 or Windows 95 if you are installing Windows 98) or from MS-DOS. You must use the version that is appropriate for your needs – the cheaper Upgrade version can be used only if you already have Windows 3.1 or 95 in use. You can alter any of the installed options later, for example, to add new printers to Windows. Even if you change the screen graphics card you do not need to go all the way through Setup again in order to ensure that you have the correct files on your hard disk.

- During installation, you will be prompted to insert a floppy to be made into a *Startup* disk. You can also make a Startup disk by using the *Add/Remove programs* option of the Control Panel, see later. This disk can be used if, for any reason, you find that Windows does not start when the computer is switched on. When you use the Startup disk the computer will start in MS-DOS, but you will be able to use diagnostic programs and to switch to the hard drive once you have sorted out any problems with it.

PRACTICAL INSTALLATION

- If you are keeping costs low, you may want to install Windows 95 rather than Windows 98, since prices for Windows 95 will drop when the 98 version is available. The notes that follow will therefore deal with the Windows 95 installation because the Windows 98 installation follows the same pattern. In addition, it may be cheaper to install Windows 95 and then use the Windows 98 upgrade than to use the full version of Windows 98. If you do not have Windows 3.1 or 95 installed on your hard drive, you must use the full version of Windows 98 to upgrade to this system.

If you are installing to a machine that uses a completely new hard drive, you will have to boot from a floppy that has the MS-DOS tracks on it, a system floppy. You should then use FDISK if the hard drive has not been partitioned, and then the FORMAT C: /SYS command to format the hard drive (unless you know that it is already formatted), and you will have to install the CD-ROM driver software so that you can make use of this drive (usually the D: drive).

If you have a hard drive that is already populated so that the computer will boot up from it, you should check that it does not cause any incompatible software to run. Such software might, for example, have been inherited from Windows 3.1. You will need to check the AUTOEXEC.BAT and CONFIG.SYS files for any entry that could cause problems. In particular you should remove UNDELETE, and VSAFE commands if they are present. To view and edit the contents of these files, use a DOS text editor such as MS-DOS Edit, and open the file C:\AUTOEXEC.BAT or C:\CONFIG.SYS, unless you know that AUTOEXEC.BAT is in another folder such as C:\DOS. Look for the lines that contain the names of programs that could cause trouble, and type the word REM ahead of the name.

For example, if you find the word VSAFE in one line, alter this to REM VSAFE. This will prevent the program from being placed in the memory, but it makes it possible to replace the program easily later by removing the REM. If either file contains a program name which is known to be totally incompatible with Windows then delete the name using the normal Notepad or Edit commands.

- Make sure that your AUTOEXEC.BAT file does not use the commands APPEND, JOIN or SUBST. Remove any lines that contain these commands.

You should then reboot the machine so that the changes to CONFIG.SYS and AUTOEXEC.BAT take effect. The machine should now be in a state that is ready for installation of Windows. Place the Windows 95 CD-ROM in its drive, or use floppy disk #1 if you have opted for the floppy set. If your machine is running Windows 3.1, make sure that only Program Manager is active.

Use the Setup command. From the CD-ROM this will use the command D:\WIN95\SETUP for the Windows 95 CD, or A:\SETUP from a floppy. You can issue this as an MS-DOS command, or from the Run command of Windows 3.1 or Start – Run of Windows 95. If you are using Windows 95 and installing Windows 98, use the Start – Run sequence, and look for the Setup program.

You are advised that Setup is preparing a Setup Wizard to guide you through the rest of the process. This takes several minutes. You will be shown a license agreement and asked to click on the *Yes* button if you agree to its terms. If you click on the *No* button Setup will be abandoned.

The Wizard now starts. Another notice appears, showing the three main stages in installation. These are:

1. Collecting information from you and from the computer.
2. Copying Windows 95/98 files to the hard drive.
3. Restarting the computer and finishing Setup.

You are reminded that installing Windows 95/98 will replace any older Windows version – this is true only if you use the same directory (folder). Stage 1 is highlighted, and clicking on the *Next* button will allow you to continue. You are asked to select the Directory (Folder), with the default of C:\WINDOWS. You can type in another folder name if you wish to keep the old Windows 3.1 system intact.

- There is no point in doing this unless you need to, for example if you want to take screenshots of the older Windows version. Almost all of the accessories and other programs that are in your old Windows folder will remain in place when Windows 95/98 is installed.

The Setup Wizard now checks for installed components and for disk space. You will be warned at this point if the disk space is inadequate. You are now asked to select which type of installation you want, with the choices of *Typical* (the default), *Compact* (for small hard drives) and *Custom*. Use *Typical* unless you particularly need to use *Compact*. Use *Custom* only if you have some experience with setting up other large software packages. Using *Typical* does not restrict your ability to make choices of the software that you will load in, and you can add to or remove portions later if you want.

You will be asked to fill in your name and (if required) company name. In the course of a *Hardware check* you will be asked to click on a box if you have a network adapter. If you click on this box Windows will try to find the type of network, and if it cannot, you will need to supply details of your network.

The other hardware is then checked. This takes several minutes of frantic disk activity, and the progress is indicated by a bar display. The rate of progress is much slower near the end, so that the time from 95% to 100% is as long as from 0% to 95%. The screen carries a notice about recovery in the eventuality of the disk activity ceasing before the end of checking.

Windows components are now checked. The default is to install the most common components, with the option to see the list of components. Whatever you do not install now can be installed from the Control Panel later, but using the option to see the list can save time later because you know exactly what you have or have not installed.

The groups that appear are headed Accessories, Communications, Disk Tools, Exchange, Fax, Multimedia and Networks, and the default disk space required is around 50 Mbyte. For each group, you can click a button to show the programs in detail, with the size for each. These are listed below for each group, with the default selection for Windows 95 shown in italics.

Accessories:

Accessibility Options (0.3M)

Briefcase (0.2M)

Calculator (0.2M)

Character Map (0.1M)

Clipboard Viewer (0.1M)

Desktop Wallpaper (0.1M)

Document Templates (0.2M)

Games (0.7M)

Mouse Pointers (0.4M)

Multi-language (2.2M)

Net Watcher (0.1M)

Object Packager (0.1M)

On-line Guide (8.2M)

Paint (1.1M)

Quick View (1.3M)

Quick View Extra (0.3M)

Screen Savers (0.1M)

System Monitor (0.1M)

Win 98 Tour (2.5M)

WordPad (1.3M)

The Accessibility Options provide assistance for handicapped users. Briefcase is used in conjunction with a portable computer to ensure that files on the portable match those held on a desktop machine. The Calculator and Character Map are as used in Windows 3.1, as are Clipboard Viewer and Desktop Wallpaper (though with new patterns).

Document Templates allow you to create new documents for your most-used programs – this item does not appear in the Help files. Mouse Pointers allows you to use new mouse pointers. Multi-language support is required only if you use Cyrillic, Turkish, Greek or Baltic languages.

Net Watcher is applicable only if you are on a network. Object Packager is required if you use object linking as in Windows 3.1. The Online Guide provides the Help pages. Paint is a replacement for the Windows Paintbrush package in Windows 3.1, and is dealt with in a later part of this book. Quick View is a utility for viewing file contents for text files, and Quick View Extra allows more file types to be viewed. Finally, WordPad is the wordprocessor that replaces the older Write as used in Windows 3.1.

Communications:

Dial-up Networking (0.4M)	*Direct Cable Connection* (0.5M)
HyperTerminal (0.4M)	*Phone Dialer* (0.1M)

Dial-up Networking allows you to network with remote computers over a modem link, and *Direct Cable Connection* allows you to link up with other computers using serial or parallel cables, as distinct from the use of networking cards. *Direct Cable Connection* cannot be selected unless you also select *Dial-up Networking*, and you will be asked for Workgroup identification. If you have used Interlink with Windows 3.1, it may be easier to retain Interlink than to try to use Direct Cable Connection.

The HyperTerminal program is the replacement for the older Windows 3.1 Terminal, allowing you to communicate with Bulletin Boards and other services obtained through the modem. Phone Dialer allows you to dial numbers from the computer, a facility that was incorporated into the Cardfile of Windows 3.1.

Disk Tools:

Backup (1M) *Defragmenter* (0.3M) *Disk Compression Tools* (0.9M)

None of these is selected as a default in the Typical installation selection. If you use Tape or Floppy backup you should install Backup, and if you have used compressed floppies in the past you should install *Disk Compression Tools* so that you can read these floppies after installing Windows 98. If you do not install Disk Compression Tools now or later, your compressed floppies will show the DRVSPACE.000 file rather than the true contents. The *Defragmenter* should be installed so that you can maintain your hard drive in good condition – unlike older versions it can be used while you are still running other programs.

Exchange:

Compuserve (0.7M)   *Microsoft Exchange* (4.5M)

Neither of these is selected by default. Use Compuserve only if you have an account with Compuserve. Microsoft Exchange is used for electronic mail, including fax, so that it must be installed if you intend to use Microsoft Fax or the Microsoft Network.

Fax: Consists of this one item, 2.1 Mbyte size. Exchange is also required. Note that you need a large memory to run Fax, preferably more than 8 Mbyte.

Multimedia:

Audio Compression (0.2M)	*Video & Sound Clips* (1.5M)
CD Player (0.2M)	*Sound Recorder* (0.3M)
Media Player (0.2M)	*Utopia Sound Scheme* (0.6M)
MusicA Sound Scheme (0.7M)	*Video Compression* (0.4M)
Nature Sound Scheme (3.1M)	*Volume Control* (0.1M)
Robotz Sound Scheme (1.8M)	

Audio Compression allows sound waves to be stored in a reasonably compact form by using compression methods. The CD Player option allows you to use your CD-ROM drive for playing music CDs. The Media Player option allows other inputs such as audio tape or video to be used. The Sound Scheme files are of pre-recorded sounds, and Video Sound Clips contain both sound and video.

The *Sound Recorder* allows you to plug a microphone or other signal source into your sound card and create sound files from your own voice or your favourite tapes or CDs. *Video Compression* allows video inputs to be compressed, and compressed video files to be used. *Volume Control* allows all sound sources to be controlled so that you do not need to use the older MS-DOS mixer controllers.

The Microsoft Network: This uses 2 Mbyte and permits you to gain access to all on-line services, including the Internet, if you sign up to the service.

Once you have selected programs to install you will be asked if you want to create a Startup disk. This is a floppy that contains the essential files (MS-DOS) that allow you some control over the computer (such as running ScanDisk) if Windows 98 fails to boot correctly. You should opt to create a Startup disk at this stage, using an ordinary 1.4 Mbyte floppy, not a DriveSpaced floppy. You can also create such floppies later if required. The Startup disk is not created at this point.

This ends the first section of the Setup procedure. In the second stage, files for a Startup disk are copied on to the hard drive. After about 20% of this has been done you will be prompted to insert a blank formatted 1.4 Mbyte floppy to configure as a Startup disk if you have taken the recommended option. After this has been done, copying resumes and if you are using floppies you will be asked to insert the appropriate disks.

The main files are then copied. During this action, you will see a Welcome screen with various reminders of the advantages of using Windows 98. You are then asked to remove all floppy disks so that the computer can be restarted (rebooted) automatically – *do not* attempt to restart using Ctrl-Alt-Del or by switching off. You should see the usual initial messages as your computer starts, and this will be followed by a screen display titled *Getting ready to run Windows 98 for the first time*.

You are informed that Configuration files are being updated, and there will be several minutes of intense disk activity. After some alternations of blank screens and picture screens, you will see a message about setting up Hardware and any Plug and Play devices. You will be asked to check the Time Zone, which should be set on the Dublin, Edinburgh, London axis for UK users. You can also check and alter time and date in this display by clicking the appropriate tab, or it can be done later in Control Panel.

If you have opted for Microsoft Exchange you will be asked (in a Wizard display) if you have used Exchange before, with the default answer of No. Several other pages of questions follow this one, allowing you options for the use of Exchange. The default options are to download mail at Startup if connected, and to accept all Internet addresses using the @ sign.

The Fax setup, if this has been selected, starts by installing the modem and checking the UK access code, your area code, and any number (such as 9) that you need to dial for an outside line from an office. You also need to select dialling method, which for most users is now Tone, the default. The modem is then installed. You will be asked to choose how to handle incoming calls, with the default that when the phone rings you will start the fax answering system manually. This is the preferred option if fax and phone share the same line. The other options are to answer automatically after four rings (this number can be changed), or to ask about answering when the phone rings. You will be asked to enter your name and fax number if you have opted to use Fax.

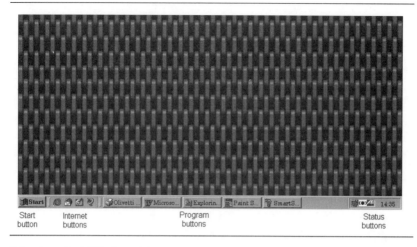

| Start button | Internet buttons | Program buttons | Status buttons |

9.1 A typical Windows 98 opening display. Programs appear on the Taskbar only if you have configured Windows to load these programs automatically.

At the end of this stage, the computer will again be restarted automatically. This restart is another slow one and you will see several messages about the final settings being made. Once this has been completed, you will be using Windows 98.

You can now see the Windows 98 Desktop display, Figure 9.1. This consists of a background (which you can alter – the example is the chain mail type) and a Taskbar at the foot which allows you to start and run programs. If you have no programs running you will see only the Start button of this display.

Before you dive in at the deep end, you should pay attention to the README and similar files. These are now easier to read, and the way in which you gain access to them is a useful introduction to Windows 98 in the following section.

NOTE: Even if you are familiar with some of the older accessories of Windows 3.1, you should read the descriptions of these utilities because they provide experience in the methods that Windows 98 uses.

WINDOW PANES – REVISION

When you start Windows 98 you will see the whole screen occupied by the blank desktop display, but when you run a program

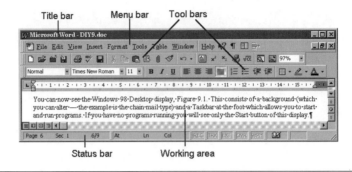

Title bar   Menu bar   Tool bars

Status bar   Working area

9.2 A typical program window – this is Microsoft Word in its 1997 version.

(application), you can opt either to use all of the screen or a portion, a window, Figure 9.2.

A typical window will consist of a rectangular area which is the working space, with rectangular strips used for icons (or *buttons*) and for messages. The top line is the *title bar*, and it always contains the control menu icon (the Microsoft symbol or program symbol such as *W* for Word) on the left and the maximize, minimize and exit (close) icons on the right. Taking the right-hand set, you click once on an icon to carry out the action. For example, clicking *once* on the maximize icon will expand the window to the full-screen size and will change the maximize icon into a restore icon (so that you can go back to the default size).

- The control menu icon can be clicked with either the mouse button to bring up a menu for changing window size or for leaving the window. Another method is to click with the right-hand mouse button.
- Clicking with the right-hand mouse button is a very fast and useful way of getting a menu that is appropriate for the place on the screen where the pointer has been placed.

Below this title bar is the *menu bar* which contains the names of the menus. There will usually be menu headings of File, Edit, View and Help, and some windows will carry other menu items which can include icons. You can click on a name to display the full menu. There is often an additional bar of icons below this. At the foot of the window there is a third bar, usually a *status bar*, which displays information about the program you are using, such as the name of a file being used.

Your first impression of Windows 98 comes from the Welcome screen with its Tip of the Day. This is the only time you will see this screen unless you opt to display it each time you switch on. If you want to see all of the Tips separately, they are available in the Help files, and you can look at them by typing Tips into the space in the Index pane of Help, see later.

THE F8 KEY OPTIONS

There is provision for selecting to start up with the older DOS system if you want to, and have retained the files. After switching the machine on, or using the Ctrl-Alt-Del key combination, you must wait until the message about Starting Windows 95/98 appears and then press the Ctrl or F8 key. You can now use number keys for menu options, some of which are used for troubleshooting, others for starting in MS-DOS.

If you are inexperienced with MS-DOS and need to know more, see the books *MS-DOS Made Simple* or the *Pocket Book of MSDOS*.

You can also use key 6 to run MS-DOS in Safe mode, which means that none of the CONFIG.SYS or AUTOEXEC.BAT file commands will be used. This is useful if you suspect that one of these commands is causing problems (as, for example, a faulty network command might) that prevent Windows from loading correctly.

The 3 key will start Windows in Safe mode, in which only the bare minimum of services operate. This is enough to allow you to sort out many of the type of problems (usually with networks) that might prevent Windows 95 from loading correctly. You should restart after sorting out the problems.

There are also the options of using key 1, for normal start (seldom needed, since this is the default if you do not press the F8 key), and for logging the start steps using the C:\BOOTLOG file. This is of interest to specialists only.

You can also start in MS-DOS by using the Startup floppy that will be made during Windows 95 setup.

When you leave Windows 95 one of the options that you will see is to go to MS-DOS. This allows you to use MS-DOS in the normal way.

● Once you have Windows installed, you need to learn the system, even if you have had previous experience of an earlier version. Take a look at the *Pocket Book of Windows 98* if this is the version that you have installed.

EXPLORER

The largest visible change in Windows 98, as compared to Windows 95, is in the Explorer. This can now be used to explore your disk drives, a local network, or the Internet, all using the same type of interface. For example, Figure 9.3 shows one configuration of the appearance of Explorer applied to the Control Panel.

The underlining indicates that a single click will open a file, and

9.3 The Control Panel of Windows 98, using one type of view.

BUILD AND UPGRADE YOUR OWN PC

you can opt to have the underlining appear only when the pointer is over an item. You can also opt for small or large icons, or to use icons in place of or along with a short description, or to use a longer description.

Using the default system, a file is selected when the pointer is placed over it, and this is indicated by the colour reversal of the text or icon. Clicking will then open the file. If you select with the Ctrl key held down you can add other files to your selection simply by pointing at each in turn. You can also select with the Shift key held down, and pointing to the first and then to the last item of a set will select the whole set. You can also use the Edit – Select All and Edit – Invert Selection commands to make selections.

With the pointer on a file, you can right click with the mouse to get a menu that consists of Open, Print, QuickView, Send To, Cut, Copy, Create Shortcut, Delete, Rename and Properties. Note that this allows renaming which cannot now be done in the Windows 95 way.

Chapter 10

Printers and modems

Printer principles

A printer is by now such an essential part of a computer system that you tend to forget that it is seldom part of a computer package. Unlike the monitor, the printer is practically always bought separately, so that your choice of printer is important, since it may outlive several computers (in the sense that the computers are replaced by newer devices but the printer is not). In addition, it is reasonable nowadays for all but the smallest system to use more than one printer or to share the use of a printer among several computers.

- Some computer packages come with a 'free' printer, and the cost of the package reflects this. The printer may not be one that you would have wanted, and you might feel that you would rather pay less for the computer package and retain the freedom to choose a printer for yourself. The other side of the coin is that a bundled printer may come at a very attractive price, very much less than you would pay for a printer bought separately.

Output on paper is referred to as *hard copy*, and this hard copy is essential if the computer is to be of any use in business applications. For word processing uses, it's not enough just to have a printer, you need a printer with a high-quality output whose characters are as clear as those of a first-class electric typewriter. For desktop publishing you will need a laser or at least an inkjet type of printer. Given that the use of a printer is a priority for the serious computer user, what sort of printers are available? The answer is any type that comes with a parallel interface, which means virtually any printer currently on sale, though some old bargain offers may have the alternative serial type of interface. The parallel type of interface, see Chapter 5, means that each bit of a byte will be signalled to the printer over a separate wire. When control wires are also added, the cable between the computer and the printer contains a large number of wires and its connectors should be well clamped into place.

The system is simple and easy to set up, you simply plug in the cable and start printing. This is due to the standardization of the connections by the printer manufacturer Centronics, so that the parallel system is often referred to as a Centronics interface, parallel port, or the Centronics parallel interface. The main problems of parallel data transfer as far as printers are concerned are of line length and the rate at which signals are sent. Each signal is a pulse, a very short, sharp change of electrical voltage, and the longer the length of the cable, the more likely it is that signals will be corrupted. This can happen in two ways. One is that the short, sharp changes of voltage are rounded out into long, smooth changes, ruining the timing of the signals. The other problem is that a signal on one line will be picked up on another line, causing an error at the printer end of the cable.

The practical effect is to restrict parallel printer leads from computers to around 2 metres, and most printer cables are only 1 m long. You can, if you need to, get around this restriction by using repeaters, amplifiers which restore the correct signals at the end of a long line, but few PC owners take this way out of a cable length problem. Serial printers require more care over the connecting cable (of fewer wires), and infinitely more fuss and bother over setting up of software. The only advantage of using a serial printer is that the cable can be longer than the usual 2 metre length specified for parallel printers. Only a few portable machines nowadays omit a Centronics port, and it's best to avoid such machines unless the price is irresistible. The main printer types currently in use for small computers are the impact dot matrix, the inkjet, and the laser printers.

The impact dot matrix printer is still available, but has fallen out of fashion. A dot matrix printer creates each character out of a set of dots, and when you look at the print closely, you can see the dot structure. The impact types mark the paper using the impact of a needle on an inked ribbon which then hits the paper. The older type of dot matrix printer used a printhead that contained nine wires or needles in a vertical line. This 9-pin, or 9-wire, printer type is still manufactured in large quantities, and some are sold at very high prices because of their particularly robust construction or high-speed printing or both.

- An impact dot matrix (DM) printer is still a necessity if you have to print several copies in one pass, using carbon paper or other forms of multi-part stationery.

24-pin printers were developed later. By using two slightly staggered vertical rows of 12 pins each, these printers can print at a high speed and with good quality. The noise level of such printers is usually higher than that of the 9-pin types, and ribbon life is shorter since so many more pins are striking the ribbon. Each pin is, incidentally, of a smaller diameter than a human hair.

There is a huge range of manufacturers, but most printers are set up so as to emulate either the IBM range of Proprinters or the Epson types – most 24-pin printers will provide emulation of the Epson LQ type. Ribbons for impact dot matrix printers are now supplied at very reasonable prices, particularly ribbons manufactured by the long-established names in typewriter ribbon supplies, such as Kores. Ribbons (or any other accessories) obtained from the printer manufacturer are always more expensive.

INKJET MACHINES

The inkjet printer, which operates by squirting tiny jets of ink at paper from a set of miniature syringes, is a close second in quality to the laser printer, though the molten toner of a laser printer is much more water resistant than the soluble ink of an inkjet, and the print from the laser printer looks much better under slight magnification with none of the 'dotty' appearance of the inkjet output. The bubblejet technology, developed by Canon and Hewlett-Packard, has been widely adopted to make printers of remarkable quality and reliability at comparatively low prices. This technology has been said to originate in the observation that a hot soldering iron laid on a hypodermic needle caused a drop of liquid to be ejected. The principle is to use a head consisting of fine jets (of a diameter narrower than a human hair) each provided with a miniature heater wire. Passing current through the heater for a jet will expel a tiny drop of ink, so that by driving these heater wires with the same form of signals as a dot matrix impact printer, the ink can be deposited in the same character patterns.

A more recent development is the piezo inkjet printer developed by Epson. The principle here is that part of the jet path is through a piezoelectric crystal (one that deforms when a voltage is applied to it), and when a voltage pulse is applied to the crystal it contracts, forcing ink from the jet. Very high-resolution figures are claimed for this type of printer, which can be remarkably noisy compared to the bubblejet types. No other manufacturer has used this principle, and Epson printers do not appear in rebadged form.

Whatever technology you go for, inkjet printers need much more attention than the impact dot matrix or laser types. The narrow jets become easily blocked, and if this cannot be cleared by using software (applying repeated pulses to force a jet clear) then the only way out is to install a new printhead. Printhead replacement is a routine operation with the bubblejet type. Some types make the ink cartridge and printhead in one unit, so that you change the printhead with each ink cartridge. The Epson types use a permanent printhead and ink cartridges are costly.

Both ink and printhead cartridges are expensive, and this can make the use of an inkjet, however attractive the price of the printer itself, more expensive to operate than a laser printer, and very much more expensive than an impact dot matrix. Another point to remember is that the very high resolution figures that you see quoted, particularly for 'photo-real' colour printing, are achieved by using specially coated paper which can cost as much as £1 per sheet.

The inkjet types are line printers and the bubblejet type are remarkably silent, most are as quiet as a laser. The speed of printing is not as high as that of the slowest laser type, but for many applications this is of little importance, and the inkjet types have the advantage that they can also print in colour. The colour inkjet printers are sold at prices that are not substantially higher than the cost of black and white, though the cost of consumables is higher. An inkjet printer is often bundled ('free') with a new computer.

If you are concerned only with black-and-white printing, you can often pick up a good bargain of an older type of inkjet that does not cater for colour. This can be economical to use if you refill the ink cartridges yourself, and the pages of the computing magazines are filled with advertisements for supplies of ink and re-inking equipment. Some types of machines are much more amenable to re-inking than others, and this is reflected in the costs of re-inking equipment. Note that many re-inking kits contain a hypodermic syringe and needle, and you may not wish such equipment in your house.

Colour inkjet machines use a black cartridge and a colour cartridge, and the colour cartridge normally contains three coloured inks, yellow, cyan and magenta. These are the primary colours for printing, and though they ought in theory to provide black by mixing, the use of a separate black cartridge is much more satisfactory. A few printers use more colours in an attempt to improve the colour quality and resolution. Some printers will not allow you to print in black unless a colour cartridge is also present, even if you never use colour. Refilling a colour cartridge is no more difficult than refilling a black one, but you have to use small amounts of three inks.

LASER PRINTERS

The laser type of printer includes variants such as LED bar printers and LCD mask printers. These are fast and silent in action, and provide the best quality for text printing and line graphics. The classic laser types are page printers, meaning that it is necessary to store a complete page of information in the memory of the printer in order to print the page. Some laser printers require 2 Mbyte or more of memory to function satisfactorily when you are printing complicated material such as DTP pages.

- The LED bar types are not page printers, and can work line by line, requiring very little memory. The mechanism is also simpler.

The quoted speed of most laser printers refers to repeated copies of a single page and does not refer to normal printing, which can be considerably slower because of the need to store the details of each page in the memory. All quoted printing speeds for printers of any kind tend to be optimistic.

Laser printers work on a principle called Xerography^{TM} which was invented by the Xerox Corporation in the 1960s. The similarities between the laser printer and the Xerox photocopier are so close that the two products can be made in one assembly line. A page cannot be printed until the drum which is used to store the 'bit image' of a page is fully 'printed' with electrical charges. The drum is usually 'printed' more than once to form a page, but the printing does not start until all the print bits are assembled in the memory. In addition, the mechanism depends on the paper being moved continually against a drum, rather than in one-line steps. The continuous movement makes the laser printer quieter than the dot matrix types.

- Note that a laser printer, like dot matrix types, cannot reproduce true halftones, because each dot that it prints is black. Halftones can be simulated by mixing black dots and white spaces, a process called dithering, but this leads to a coarse appearance on a 300 dots per inch printer and is really satisfactory only on a typesetting machine which works at 1200 to 2400 dots per inch. Dithering is also used with colour inkjet machines to create colours other than the yellow, cyan and magenta used in colour printing.

Paper is the most consumed item, and laser printers use, as might be expected, the photocopier grade of paper whose cost is at least twice that of ordinary paper of the same density unless you shop around. The reason for the additional cost is because of the way the toner is deposited on to the paper. The paper should consist of fibres which are all aligned along the longer axis of the paper, making the paper behave more uniformly when subject to electric charges (and discharges). It also allows the paper to feed through the machine with less tendency to curl. In addition, since the toner is fixed to the paper by fairly intense heating, the paper must not darken or curl when it is heated. These requirements make the paper more expensive to produce, though some shopping around can reveal better prices than can be obtained from local suppliers. Try Viking Direct if you cannot obtain low-cost paper locally – and look at their catalogue also when you want other consumables like toner. Most local office suppliers, however, are able to provide copier paper at around £3 per ream (500 sheets). This grade of paper is also suitable for black inkjet use.

Whatever is claimed by manufacturers, the use of very heavy (more than 90 grams per square metre) and expensively finished paper is not justifiable. Such paper will often feed badly, forming ridges, and will allow toner to smear. Very heavy paper will stick in the printer or cause loud protests from the rollers. Lighter and more absorbent papers usually produce better results – try cheap grades first and always try a sample before you buy several hundred packs.

The main consumables of laser printers, other than paper, are the toner and the drum. The toner is a dry ink that can be melted on to the paper by heated rollers after the paper has picked up the powder from another roller. The drum is a roller coated with a material that is light sensitive, and it is the action of a laser beam, or light from other sources, that causes this drum to become electrically charged and retain a pattern of toner. The toner comes in a cartridge, and for printers that use a separate drum and toner cartridge, several cartridges of toner can be used before the drum has to be replaced. The Hewlett-Packard models use a combined drum and toner cartridge, so that renewing this cartridge ensures that you are using new parts for all the consumable items.

- There are some types of printers which are classed as laser printers but which do not use a laser beam. These are LED bar or LCD mask types which use the same principles of light beams affecting a charged drum, but without the use of a laser beam scanning over the drum. These types are not page printers, and can work line by line, requiring very little memory.

The quoted speed of most laser printers, 4 pages per minute upwards, refers to printing repeated copies of a single page and does not refer to normal printing, which is always very much slower. This is because a substantial amount of the time that is needed for printing consists of building up the instructions in the memory for forming the charge pattern on the drum, and if this pattern remains fixed, page printing can be as fast as the speed of the drum permits. When each page is different, and in particular if graphics images are used on each page, the time needed to form the pattern makes the printing rate very much slower. All quoted printing speeds for printers of any kind tend to be highly optimistic. The fastest printing is of pages of text that use one of the built-in fonts of the printer.

Photo-real printing

The growing popularity of digital cameras, which should eventually cause a gradual increase in resolution figures and an equal decrease in prices, will create a demand for printers that can perform colour printing of photographic standards. At the time of writing, digital cameras in general do not have sufficient resolution to match the smallest and cheapest film camera, but this and other aspects (such as interchangeable lenses) of digital photography should improve in time. The attraction of these cameras is that the image can be edited, so that you can remove red-eye effects or the tree that always seems to grow out of someone's head. The camera, however, has to be matched by a printer to make use of these actions.

Many types of inkjet printers claim photo-real performance, and using coated paper they can produce results as good as the colour illustrations in newspapers. If you want printing that more closely approaches the prints from film, however, other printer types are preferable, and at the present time the dye sublimation type is by far the most realistic option. The prices are already quite low in the USA, and eventually they may be low even in the UK, which is traditionally the place where prices can be maintained high for the longest time.

The advantage lies in the way that colours other than the primary yellow, cyan and magenta are produced. Inkjets produce other colours by dithering, spraying the paper with dots of different primary colours. Dye sublimation printers use vaporized inks, and these can be mixed before they hit the paper so that each dot is of the correct colour with no need to dither. One figure that is often used is that a 300 dot per inch dye sublimation printer produces results equivalent to a 5000 dot per inch inkjet. This is much closer to photographic resolution than can be achieved by conventional inkjet machines, and if you want to work with high-quality images you should consider the use of this type of printer for your images, perhaps using a cheap inkjet or laser printer for text.

Modems and serial communications

The modem is a device that makes use of a serial port to transmit or receive data one bit at a time. When data is sent one bit at a time, some method has to be used to allow the receiving computer (or other device) to distinguish one group of eight bits (a byte) from its neighbour. This problem does not exist for a parallel system, because in the instant when a character is transmitted, all of its bits exist together as signals on the eight separate lines. For a serial transmission there is just one line for the bits of data, and the eight data bits must be sent in turn and assembled into a byte by storing them at the receiving end. The problem is that since one bit looks like any other, how does the receiving machine recognize the first bit of a byte?

The way round the problem is to precede each transmitted byte of eight bits by a start bit (a zero) and end it by either one or two stop bits (each a 1). Notice that once again there is no standardization of the number of stop bits, though one stop bit is slowly becoming the more common practice. Ten (or 11) bits must therefore be transmitted for each byte of data, and both transmitter and receiver must use the same number of stop bits. The transmitting computer will send out its bytes of data, and at the receiving computer, the arrival of a start bit will start the machine counting in the bits of data. These are stored then into its memory until there is a set of eight, and then the computer checks that it has the correct number of stop bits after the last data bit. If the pattern of a zero, then eight bits (0 or 1), then a 1, is not found (assuming eight data bits and one stop bit), then the receiving computer can be programmed to register a mistake in the data. This will start the counting action again, looking back at the stored data and starting with the next 0 bit that could be a start bit. The recounting is fast, and can be carried out in the time between the arrival of one bit and the next, so that it would be unusual to miss more than one character in this way. All of this is the task of the communications software that you

50	75	110	150	Slow, seldom used
300	600	1 200	2 400	Printers and modems
4800	9600			Modems and fax
19 200	28 800	33 600		Voice/fax modems
56 000				Now standardized as V90

10.1 Standard speeds – only the faster speeds are in use nowadays.

use with each computer and is carried out automatically if, and only if, you have programmed the software to work with the correct settings.

The use of the same number of stop bits and data bits by both computers is not in itself enough to ensure correct transfer, though. In addition to using the same number of data bits and stop bits, both transmitter and receiver must work with the same number of bits per second. In the (rather loose) language of computer communications, they must use the same baud rate. Baud rate and bits per second are not necessarily identical, but that's something for the experts to worry about. Quoted figures for the speed of communications always use the phrase baud rate to mean the number of bits per second, and we'll stick with that to avoid confusion. Figure 10.1 shows the RS-232 standard bit rates, of which 300, 1200, 2400 and 9600 are the older standards, hardly ever used nowadays.

For most practical purposes you can take the baud rate as meaning the number of bits per second, so that the number of characters per second is equal to the baud rate divided by the total number of bits in each byte. If, for example, you use a start bit, eight data bits and one stop bit, you have a total of ten bits per byte, and at 1200 baud you will be sending 120 characters per second. It's certainly faster than you can type, but at this speed you will need a time of around 200 seconds (3.3 minutes) to transmit a 4000 word article. The timer will be ticking away inside the telephone exchange for all this time, plus the time it has taken you to make sure that transmission has been established. Do not consider a modem slower than 33 Kbit/s, though at a pinch if you do not need fast Internet access you can get 28.8 Kbit/s modems at low prices.

Good software can make use of methods of adding data so as to provide for better checking and can even provide for the correction of errors to some extent. The checking methods can range from the simple checksum system to the very complicated Reed–Solomon system (also used in compact discs), but they all have one factor in common, redundancy. All checking involves sending more bits or bytes than the bytes of the data, with the extra bits or bytes carrying checking and error-correcting signals. Some of these can work on individual bytes, even on individual bits; others are intended to work on complete blocks of 128 bytes or more. The checksum, for example, works by adding the number values of all of the ASCII codes in a set number of bytes, often 128. This sum is transmitted as a separate byte, and at the receiver the codes are again summed and the total compared with the transmitted checksum. Only if the two match will the set of bytes be accepted.

Because these checking methods all involve the transmission of extra bytes, they slow down the rate of communication of useful data. For text transmissions, the use of elaborate checking is often unnecessary because an occasional mistyped character in text is often not important compared to the need for a high speed of transmission. For sending program files, however, one false byte is usually enough to ensure that the program does not run correctly, so that much better checking methods must be used even if this means taking longer to transmit the data. You often have to select, by way of your communications software, different methods for transmitting different types of data. If you use communications for purely business purposes you are likely to be concerned mainly with exchanging text rather than program files, but you might need to use exchange methods that employed checking if you transmitted, for example, your Lotus 1-2-3 data files from one office to another.

PROTOCOLS

The individual items of number of data bits, number of stop bits and the use of even, odd or no parity make up what we call the modem serial *protocols*. You can't get very far in communications without knowing something about protocols, because unless both the transmitter and the receiver are using identical protocols there will be no communication, and only gibberish will be received. There is no single protocol that is used by everyone, so you need to be able to set your communications software to the protocol that is being used by the machine to which you want to be linked. Modern software makes this considerably easier than it used to be, but you still need to know what protocols are being used by the computer with which you are trying to communicate. Communications is just about the last part of computing in which you cannot bridge a gap in technical knowledge with clever software, though as we shall see, it is possible to use software that requires only an initial effort from you.

Given that the transmitter and the receiver are set up to the correct protocols, meaning that the baud rate, the number of stop bits and the use of parity will be identical, we still need some method of handshaking to ensure that signals are transferred only when both transmitter and receiver are ready. You might, for example, be recording data on your disk as it arrived, so that there would have to be a pause in the reception of signals while the disk system got into action. Another possibility is that you are printing out the data as it is transmitted, and your printer operates at a speed slower than the baud rate of the transmission. Whatever the reason, just to have transmitter and receiver working at the same rate is not enough, because you also have to ensure that the bits are in step at all times, and you have to make it possible to pause now and again without any loss of data. A serial link to a printer can make use of 'hardware handshaking' meaning that the handshaking can be implemented by using electrical signals over another set of lines, but this option is not open to most communications applications because we can't use extra telephone lines.

The handshaking is therefore implemented in software by using the XON/XOFF system. This uses the ASCII code numbers 17 and 19, which are not used for characters, sent between one computer and the other. Data can be sent out from a computer following the ASCII 17 code, and disabled following the ASCII 19 code. Since these codes are sent over the normal data lines, no additional electrical connections are needed. The rate of data transfer is slower because of the time that is needed to send the XON/XOFF signals, so that if you organize your system in such a way that the least use of handshaking occurs, you will transmit or receive faster. The use of XON/XOFF is by far the most common method of software handshaking that is used in communications (another system is called EIA).

- Do not be put into a state of panic by a manual that comes with a modem, because these are intended for designers rather than for users. All you normally have to do is to connect up the modem and run the appropriate software. Most modem users want Internet connection, and once the modem is connected you simply use the CD provided by your Internet Provider (IP) and take it all from there.

COMPUTER TO COMPUTER

Suppose we had two computers, which could be of any two types, in the same room or the same building and we wanted to transfer data between them, despite the fact that they used different disk formats. If each computer has a serial port, the input/output connector for serial signals, then all that is needed is a cable to join these ports. If the cable can be bought or made to order (it would have to be of the non-modem or DTE to DTE type) then comparatively simple software could be used to transfer data that was entirely composed of ASCII codes. Almost any kind of communications software could be used to make the task considerably easier. The INTER-LINK of MS-DOS 6.0 allowed a simple serial link like this to be used as a form of network, and Windows 95 and 98 contain software called Direct Cable Connection, see later, which is easier to use. The methods that we use for more remote computers all centre on the use of a modem.

Consider for a moment the achievement of Alexander Graham Bell in 1876, which he beneficently intended as an aid for the deaf, but which we now call the telephone. The telephone system, now as then, is intended to transmit the electrical signals that are obtained from a microphone operated by the human voice. Like any other waves, the waves of sound of the voice cover a range of frequencies, meaning the number of vibrations per second. In honour of the pioneer of radio, Heinrich Hertz, the unit of one vibration per second is called the hertz, abbreviated to Hz. The range of frequencies that is needed for intelligible (as distinct from high-quality) speech transmission is quite small, of the order of 300 to 3000 vibrations per second, usually written as 300–3000 Hz. By contrast, the transmission of music of the quality that we get on a good recording demands (but seldom gets) a range of frequencies from about 30 Hz to 18 000 Hz, and television pictures require a range from zero hertz to 5.5 million hertz because of their complicated pattern.

The equally spiky signals from a computer also, even if they are slowed down to a low speed of 300 per second or lower, simply cannot be transmitted through a telephone circuit. What we need is a device that detects a computer ON signal and turns it into one tone and will similarly turn an OFF signal into another tone, or a tone that is different from the first in some way, like being out of step. The action of converting the computer signals into tones is called *modulation*, and we must be able also to carry out the opposite action which is called *demodulation*. The combining of the words modulation and demodulation gives us the word *modem*, which is the name of the device that carries out this transformation. The modem is connected to the computer by a serial link, using normal hardware handshaking, but the lead out from the modem to the outside world is a single lead, suitable for telephone connection, using XON/XOFF handshaking.

For most purposes, you need to use a modem that will work in both directions at the same time (full duplex) so that just altering one tone is not enough, and you need to be able to work with two. For low baud rates, it's possible to have four different tones in use, two for transmitting and two for receiving, with the actual frequency of the tones carefully chosen so as not to cause problems with the telephone system itself. Most telephone systems around the world use different tones to represent the different dialled numbers, and even in the UK where the old pulse system (one pulse for one, two pulses for two and so on) is still used for domestic telephones, the tone system is used between exchanges.

For the higher baud rates the use of separate tones is not possible. You cannot carry a signal of 2000 baud with a frequency that is lower than 2000 Hz. Because the higher baud rates are much too close to the upper limit of frequency than the telephone lines can cope with there is no possibility of using four tones each higher than the baud rate and each separable from the other. The faster modems therefore use a system of phase shifting, meaning that the frequency is unchanged but a change is represented by a shift (called a *phase shift*) of the signal, as illustrated in Figure 10.2. This allows a signal of comparatively low frequency to carry several thousand changes per second, so that a rate of 2000 bits per second can be carried with a signal that need be sampled only 600 times per second. This is where baud rate and bits per second become different, and the established practice as far as computer communications are concerned is to refer to the rate in bits per second as the baud rate. As a computer user, the number of bits per second is the important figure for you, the true baud rate is the figure of importance to the telephone line engineer. The more modern telephone exchanges which are installed all over the country will cope with these phase shift signals. In the few places where the old fashioned 1910 style (that's the date of invention, not the type number) of automatic exchange is still in use, you can use only the slower baud rates.

Now at this point it's important to clear up yet another misuse of words that creates a lot of problems for users. Practically all modems that are used for computer communications are *full duplex*, using one set of frequencies (or frequency change) to transmit and another to receive. A full-duplex *modem* attached to one computer must be connected through the telephone lines to another full duplex modem at the other end, because if it were not then the frequencies or frequency changes would not match. If you had a full-duplex modem connected to a half-duplex modem (using the same

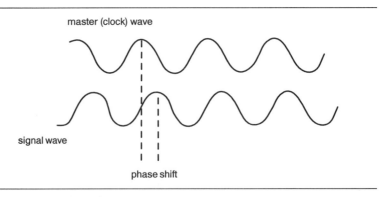

10.2 Using phase shift. Each different phase angle can be interpreted as a set of bits, so that, for example, using four phase can be used to code the bit pairs 00, 01, 10 and 11. Using eight phase angles allows three-bit numbers to be encoded, and 16 phase will code four-bit numbers.

frequencies for transmitting and for receiving) then it could receive the signals from the full-duplex modem but could not transmit to it.

The confusion arises because the terms full duplex and half duplex are applied also to software that controls the use of the modem. A lot of services that you contact with your full-duplex modem will echo back your signal as you send it so that a copy appears on your screen. Software should refer to this as remote echo, but sometimes calls it full duplex. Other services do not carry out this remote echo, and your software may instruct you to switch to half duplex, meaning local echo (so that what you type is put on to your screen by your own computer rather than by the remote computer). Your modem, however, will be operating with full duplex, though the software may not be using the transmitted and the received signals at the same time.

The modem is therefore a very necessary intermediate between the computer and the telephone lines, allowing computers to be connected together so as to transfer data no matter how far apart the computers happen to be. Modern PC machines can have a modem added in card form. Other modems can be connected to the computer by way of a cable from the serial port, and such a modem would need this serial connection, a mains cable connection and a telephone connection in order to work. When you use the internal modem, only the telephone cable requires to be connected into a telephone socket of the BT standard type. Beware, incidentally, of modems that are not BT approved. They may be cheap, but if BT cuts off your line because it has discovered that you are using a non-approved modem you will be charged again for reconnection. An even nastier prospect is the refusal of an insurance company to pay out after a fire if non-approved equipment has been in use.

Before you start to be too optimistic about the prospects, however, you need to know a lot more about modems. To start with, there are a huge number of modems available, mainly because speed capabilities keep changing. Nowadays, you should not contemplate using any modem that was slower than 28.8 kbit/s, and preferably you would go for one that was a fax modem and a voice modem. A fax modem allows you to send and receive fax (there are still places that do not use E-mail). A voice modem allows you to pass voice messages (converted to digital signals) along the Internet, allowing you to phone anyone with suitable equipment anywhere in the world at the price of a local call.

Most modems are capable of working at rates that are much faster than any you can use over the public telephone lines. This is because you might want to use modems for computer to computer transmissions within a building, using internal lines, or over an internal telephone exchange that can cope with higher frequencies. Even if the modem is internal you still have a serial link between the computer and the modem, and you need to know at what rates this can be used. Your software will refer to serial 'ports', meaning the connections through which serial data can be transmitted and received. These are distinguished by using COM1 to refer to the port connector at the back of the PC, and (usually) COM3 to refer to the internal port that is part of an internal modem. If you use an external modem, you also need to use COM1 or COM2. Problems that used to arise when more than two serial ports are used have now been resolved for anyone using an up-to-date motherboard and using Windows 95 or Windows 98.

BAUD RATES AND OTHER PROTOCOLS

We have seen already that a serial transmission allows signals to be sent over a single line, such as a telephone line. These signals are sent bit by bit, using 7 or 8 bits per character byte along with a start bit and either one or two stop bits in each byte. The most favoured set at present is 8 data bits with one start bit and one stop bit, but you have to use whatever system is favoured by the device at the other end of the line, because there is no agreed universal standard. The baud rate that is quoted for modems or software is (in practical terms at least) the number of bits per second. Using 8 data bits with one start and one stop bit makes a total of ten bits for each character byte, so that a baud rate of 28 800 means 2880 characters per second.

These rates are usually referred to by modem manufacturers in a different way, using the type numbers such as V21, V22, V22-bis and V23, and these designations indicate that a modem is an old one, unsuited to modern use. The more recent modems are likely to be V34 (28 800 bits per second) or V34+ (33 600 bits per second), and the most recent modems use a rate of 56 000 bits per second. At the time of writing, the standard for this fast rate had just been agreed as the V90 specification. See under *Fast modems* at the end of this chapter.

A faster rate of data exchange can be obtained by using an ISDN (Integrated Signals Digital Network) connection. This requires a special line that is expensive to install and rent, and it needs a different form of modem in the computer. The benefit is that it allows fast communication and is particularly suitable if you want to leave the computer running on communications 24 hours per day, or if you want to send sound and video data from one place to another.

Internet use of a modem can run up large telephone bills, even with a provider that uses a local call number which is placed on your BT Family and Friends list. Cable TV providers can often offer both telephone and Internet facilities at lower prices, and to my mind this service is a lot more appealing than the TV programs on offer. You may, however, have to take a package of TV channels in order to get the useful stuff. Another possibility that looks promising at the time of writing is Internet connection by way of the electricity supply cables.

OTHER MODEM FEATURES

What other modem features should you be aware of? One facility that is provided on practically every modern modem at any price range is auto-answer, meaning that the modem will accept calls automatically. In other words, while you have your computer switched on and your communications software working, an incoming call will be put through to the computer without the need for you to lift a telephone receiver. This allows your computer to act rather like an answering machine, but without your voice being heard by the caller, and it is handy if you expect data to be sent to you while you are out. The auto-answer modem will provide the correct signal to the remote transmitter that you are connected, using the same type of signal as would be sent by lifting a handset. Remember, however, that there is no point in receiving messages while you are out unless your software provides for passing such software to a disk file as 'voice mail'. In addition, if messages can be sent to you while you are out, it may also be possible for a caller to read what is on some files in your disk. The more elaborate communications software will allow only a limited number of files to be read unless a special password is used to gain access to disk commands (commands that are often termed 'shell' commands because they are carried out by the operating system or shell, usually MS-DOS).

Another feature which appears on many, but not all, modern modems is auto dial. As the name suggests, this allows you to carry out dialling without the use of a separate handset, and it's a very useful facility even if you are only going to use a voice transmission. To be able to dial numbers automatically requires that the modem can issue either pulses (for the old UK system) or tones (almost universal now). If you are buying a modem that you will be using for some time to come it's wise to get one that can use either pulse or tone, selected either manually or automatically. If the auto dial system is described as 'Hayes' then it conforms to the standards laid down by the Hayes Corporation, the (US) leader in modem design. Using an auto dial modem opens the door to the use of software that stores and selects telephone numbers. You can, for example, store up to 100 telephone numbers with some types of software and dial up any number simply by requesting a name. In addition, most suitable software will provide for redialling an engaged number (currently frowned on by BT) and for providing your password(s) when the other machine answers.

The third common and very useful facility is auto detect, also called auto scan. A modem fitted with this facility can detect what baud rate is being used by the remote machine, and set itself accordingly, so that you never have to bother about setting a baud rate for yourself. This is particularly useful if you use an auto dial system with a lot of different numbers that use different baud rates. It does not, however, automatically set the number of data bits or stop bits for you, so that there is still something to do for yourself. Suitable software will allow you to keep a file of contacts that includes all of this data so that you never have to key it in more than once.

Other features are of more interest for specialized applications. Some modems allow a set of very fast baud rates for the few users who have access to ISDN data transmission lines. A few types feature built-in error detection and correction systems, but this is just as easily provided by software. Unless your needs are rather specialized, then a comparatively simple modem will be sufficient for both business and leisure communications, but simple doesn't mean crude, and modems at bargain prices can provide all the facilities we have looked at here.

SEPARATE MODEMS

If you intend to buy a modem in the near future, then an internal modem for the PC is still by far the best buy, and is always cheaper than an external modem because it does not need a separate power supply or casing. You may, however, have a modem already or be attracted by a particularly good offer on a modem and its software. Such a modem is likely to be one of the external type which has to be connected to the PC by way of the serial port. This will have a lead that can be plugged directly into a modern BT connector socket – avoid anything that uses any other type of connection.

The separate modem requires three connections to be made. One of these is the connection to the BT telephone point, and this is usually made through a 'piggy-back' adapter so that you can still plug an ordinary telephone into the socket. You will also need a mains lead to supply power to the modem, with a 3 A fuse in the plug. Very often, the plug is part of the power supply, and no fuse is accessible. The third connector is a serial cable to connect the modem to the serial interface on the back of the PC. A cable of this type will probably be packaged with the modem and in any case is easy to get hold of because the PC serial interface wiring is as near to a standard as you are likely to find in this communications business. If you feel tempted to make up your own cable, then get a copy of the connection diagram at each end, along with a magnifying glass, a soldering iron and a set of worry beads. You'll need them.

If you have bought the cable, though, you only have to plug in at the PC end and at the modem end, put the mains plug into its socket, and the telephone plug into the BT socket, and you are ready to go. This assumes that you have suitable software in the form of a communications program or, more likely, an Internet connection. The use of an external modem in this way ties up the serial port (known as COM1 or AUX1) on your computer so that you can't use it for anything else such as a serial printer. In addition, you will need to consult your modem manual to see if any switches on the modem have to be set. Most modern modems have their settings determined entirely by the software that is used to control them, so that there are no switches (or none that you need use, at any rate) to set.

Modems are now available (as external units only) that will accept incoming fax messages and voice calls and store them independently of the computer. You can then retrieve these when you next boot up the computer. This type of modem is the perfect answer to a modern problem – the remote fax machine that has been programmed to ring your number (whether you have a fax machine or not) at odd times of day or night (usually selling double-glazing). This type of modem allows you to find who is sending the junk fax so that you can contact BT to have the nuisance ended.

FAST MODEMS

The fastest speed available in conventional (analogue) modems is 56 000 bits per second, but until mid-1998 there was no agreed standard so that two incompatible types were being sold. There is now an agreed standard called V90, and if you want to use this modem speed you should buy a V90 modem. Owners of either of the earlier types should be able to upgrade by downloading software over the Internet and installing it into the flash ROM of the modem. Make sure before you upgrade that your Internet provider can offer you connection at V90 speed and protocols.

Chapter 11

Getting more

No computer is up to date for long, and the relentless chase for more powerful software drives the hardware designers to provide more power, more memory, and more hard drive space with each month that passes. This chapter is devoted to tips for getting more speed from your existing hardware and software and to the hardware upgrades that will enhance speed.

Hardware

Memory. Adding memory is one certain way of increasing Windows running speed unless you are already using 64 Mbyte of RAM. If you need more speed and you are using 8 or 16 Mbyte then a memory upgrade to 32 Mbyte will make a considerable difference to Windows 98 speed, more than you could get by most other methods. Look out for new memory chip sets that can increase memory access speed – some might not be applicable because you cannot install them (if they use different sockets) but others might be useful if you can justify the cost of replacing all your existing memory chips. Remember that you should use matching memory types – if you use EDO SIMM for part of the memory you should use the EDO SIMM for the rest, unless you can also use a DIMM.

Faster processor. Using a faster processor is a more costly upgrade, because the price of a new processor depends heavily on how fast it is and how long it has been in production. Changing a processor is easy if the existing one uses Socket-7, and this is a feature that might keep Socket-7 in favour for some time, because not everyone wants to have to change the whole motherboard to get a faster processor. At the time of writing, the 233 MHz processors cost less than £100, making it worthwhile to remove a 166MMX chip and put in the faster processor. You should regard the fan as part of the chip, and put a new fan on the new processor (remember to mark the pin 1 position at the corner of the fan). Faster Socket-7 chips are already available (typically 266 MHz and 300 MHz), and you may feel that a Pentium-II board will be appropriate for your next computer, allowing the use of 400 MHz (or higher) chips.

New hard drive. At some stage you will want a larger capacity hard drive, and at the same time you might want to look for a faster hard drive. The access time of the drive, typically 11 ms, is a good guide to raw speed, but the performance is also affected by the size of cache memory, typically 128 or 256 Kbyte. A factor that greatly affects raw speed is the rotational speed, and spin rates of 7200 and more are now available. If your EIDE drive is not of the type marked UDMA (Ultra Direct Memory Access) then you can get appreciably faster results by changing to a drive that is of this class. Eventually, all drives will conform to this standard, but at the time of writing several do not and are appreciably slower in use. Hard drive space is particularly important if you work with photo-real images because these require a large amount of space, typically 10 Mbyte or more.

DMA settings. DMA is Direct Memory Access, and it means that bundles of data can be transferred between disk and memory with very little intervention on the part of the main processor chip. Modern hard drives, see above, can use Ultra DMA for very fast transfer, and you should make certain that fast DMA transfer is specified on your computer if the motherboard provides for it and if bus mastering is used. You can probably take it for granted that a new machine will provide the latest version, UDMA, but you may not be so certain about older machines. You can test an older machine as follows, but note that this may not check out on a new machine.

On machines manufactured since early 1997, the version of Windows 95 has been labelled 4.00.950b. To check this, select My Computer in Windows Explorer and click the File – Properties item. If your computer was new at any time later than June 1997 it is almost certain that this version will be in use. This is the OSR2 version, see earlier, and you can confirm this by looking at the Properties panel for the hard drive, which should carry the label FAT32. This late version of Windows 95 is very similar in important respects to Windows 98. If you have installed Windows 98 these settings will already have been made.

On a computer using the later Windows 95 version, you can speed up access to the hard drive and to the CD-ROM drive by enabling DMA (Direct Memory Access). This is done by starting Control Panel, and clicking in succession System, Device Manager and Disk Drives. The Disk Drives section should show both the floppy and the hard drive, with the hard drive usually identified as IDE, possibly with Type 46. Click this line, and then click on the Properties button. Click Settings, and look for a box labelled DMA. If this is not ticked, click on it. When you leave the Settings panel you will be asked to reboot the computer.

When your computer is running again, go back to the Device Manager and this time find your CD-ROM name. Click the Properties – Settings and locate the DMA box. Click this to place a tick in the box, and carry on to the reboot stage as before. By ensuring that these DMA boxes are ticked, you can speed up these actions of loading and saving, and since these are critical to overall speed of the computer, you should gain in better performance. These options are not available in earlier versions of Windows, on machines without bus mastering or on some motherboards. If the DMA box does not appear, then you cannot take this option. This does not necessarily mean that your system is not using UDMA, because on recent machines there is no indication in these Control Panel panes.

Graphics cards. The time that is needed to change the screen image counts for a lot when you are using Windows, and is even more important if you want to display fast-moving video images, particularly if these images are full-screen. For optimum Windows

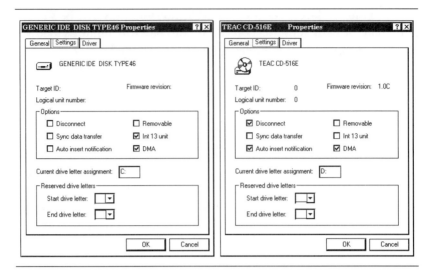

11.1 The DMA boxes for hard drive and CD-ROM drive.

performance you should be using a fast graphics card, preferably in an AGP slot, but for video performance you need even higher performance, and a card that can cope with full-screen video will not be cheap, and must use a PCI slot. You will have to decide for yourself if the cost is worth the features that the card provides. Remember that some cards that are marginally suitable with 2 Mbyte installed will be much faster with 4 Mbyte, and some cards can provide for even more video memory.

Screen use. If you are using higher resolution, such as 800×600, remember that this involves a much larger number of screen points than 640×480. The ratio is 480 000 to 307 200, around 1.56, so that you can expect a speed gain of this order if you change to the lower resolution. The potential speed gains from changing to lower colour numbers are equally impressive if you are experiencing speed problems, because dealing with 4 bits per point (16 colours) is much faster than dealing with 24 bits per point (16 million colours). Note that you will not necessarily find speed gains if your system can cope adequately with the higher resolution and colour numbers.

Software

Embellishments. You may like animated cursors and other fancy effects, but since they all demand the use of the same processor, they will inexorably slow down your system. If speed is important you should be ruthless with everything that is not strictly necessary. Taken to this logical extreme, we would all be using a different operating system, but you may find that you can live without the Tool-Tips, tip of the day, animated cursors and other items that make unwanted demands on the processor.

Software versions. Each time a new software version is announced, new features are added, and the usual result is to make the software run slower. For example, Word-6 runs at a reasonable rate on a 486/66 machine, but using Word-8 (Word 97) on the same machine is almost impossible because of the long waits for some actions (such as changing style) to take place. Word-8 needs a much faster machine, at least a 166MMX Pentium, to run it at a reasonable rate.

This suggests that you can often obtain a considerable speed advantage by using an older version of software, as you probably know if you are able to run both Windows 95 and Windows 3.1 on the same older machine. Whether you can get along with an older version or not is a matter for your judgement. Sometimes new versions incorporate great benefits and it would be difficult to return to the older version. In other examples, the newer version incorporates cosmetic changes or changes that are totally irrelevant to your needs, and the speed of the older version is much more useful than the fancy displays of the later version, often referred to as bloatware.

Too many programs. Because Windows allows you to juggle with several programs running together does not mean that you are forced to do this. Unless you have fitted a generous amount of memory, you will gain in speed by restricting the number of programs you keep running. Remember that if you force the computer to use virtual memory (see below) this will result in a large amount of hard drive activity and cause the program swapping action to be slow even if you are using a fast hard drive.

- Note that if a program running in Windows 95 or Windows 98 shows the hourglass icon to indicate that it is taking time over some action you can switch to another program in another window and continue with that one – a hangup on one program does not affect another program.

Virtual memory. Virtual memory means the use of the hard drive as if it were part of the RAM memory, and it is particularly important if you are trying to use Windows with an inadequate amount of RAM. Virtual memory is usually organized by Windows, on the basis that if you start running more programs than will fit in the available RAM, a hard drive temporary file is created to take the overspill, and data is swapped between RAM and hard drive. This involves two time-consuming actions, the creation and deletion of a temporary file, and the saving and loading hard drive actions.

One way around this if you have inadequate RAM is to create a permanent swap file. This can be done using the Control Panel, clicking the System item. In the Performance pane, click Virtual Memory, and then click on the option to manage your own virtual memory. By default, this will use the hard drive, and you can type in figures for minimum and maximum swap file size. Typical figures, assuming a large hard drive, are 64 Mbyte minimum and 256 Mbyte maximum, but if you are working with a small amount of RAM you can go for smaller amounts such as 32 Mbyte minimum and 64 Mbyte maximum.

- Do not use the option to disable swapping altogether even if you are working with 64 Mbyte or more of RAM. Windows will usually contrive to use all the RAM that you can provide.

Background saving/printing. Background working means that program actions can be carried out at a reduced rate while other software is being used. The two most important background options are background printing and background drive actions. Background printing (spooling) is standard with Windows 95 and Windows 98, and it is controlled from the Printer properties pane, using the General tab and the Spooling button. You can turn off background printing by using the *Print direct to printer* option.

Background saving is not an option in Windows, but it can be implemented in Microsoft Word-97 from the Tools – Save menu. The effect is to allow you to continue with Word even when a document is being saved, but on modern computers with fast drives the hard drive actions are so fast that in many cases the use of background saving is unnecessary.

Size of windows. The size of a window has an effect on the speed of a program that is run in that window, particularly if a slow graphics card is used. This is particularly applicable to a window whose contents are continually changing, and this is why a special accelerator card is needed if you want to display video on a large window.

Slow actions. Some actions are inherently slow, and there is very little that you can do about it. Updating very large worksheets and carrying out sorting actions on large databases can take a considerable time, and these actions are best left to carry on in the background while you work with another program. Minimize the window that contains the slow-acting program, and work on other programs until the slow action is completed. See below for slow Internet actions.

Sounds and videos. Sound and video applications both use large data files. You can save time marginally by opting not to use sound with program actions, and confining its use only to multimedia work that demands the use of sound (such as reading and listening to an article on a musical instrument). Sound is dealt with mainly by the sound card independently of the main processor, so that the time savings that are made by opting out of sound are not large, but if the continual noises are annoying the silence can be very welcome.

Video is another application that uses very large files – take a look at the size of the AVI files that accompany Windows. Processing video information requires a fast processor working almost full time on the video, so that you can expect the computer to work slowly if you are trying to run video on the full screen. If this is unacceptably slow, use a small window or fit a video accelerator card that will allow faster processing of video.

Speeding up the Net. Using the Internet is the most time-consuming aspect of computer use. This is partly because of the time needed to send information across telephone lines at a comparatively slow speed, and partly because of the way that the Web is organized. Web organization requires you to go from one link to another to find what you want and to repeat the process when you are retracing your steps.

The most obvious way to speed up Net action is to fit the fastest modem that can be used, or to use a cable connection. At the time of writing there are two incompatible 56K modem specifications and modems that are being sold for this speed contain flash-ROM that can be altered by using downloaded data now that the V90 specification has been agreed. Some Internet providers permit the use of both varieties, others settle for one or the other, so that you cannot be certain if you buy a 56K modem that you will be able to use it at that speed. At this stage it is better to wait for a certified V90 modem, and fit it when your Internet Provider can connect using V90. Developments in other ways of linking to the Internet may eventually make obsolete the use of telephone lines for this purpose.

Another aid to faster Internet use concerns what you want to obtain. If your use of the Net is mainly textual, concerned with words rather than pictures and sounds, you can speed up the action considerably by opting not to download picture, video or sound data. Using the version of Internet Explorer in Windows 98, this is done by clicking View – Internet Options and looking in the *Advanced tab*. This contains a set of selection buttons marked:

Show pictures	Play animations	Play videos
Play sounds	Smart image dithering	

and you can obtain much faster running if you leave all five of these unselected. On a Web page, the position of an image is indicated by an icon and you can right click and select *Show picture* to see the image if you think it might be useful. If you find that pictures are really needed you can click this option – some Web pages contain option buttons that are images and cannot be used so easily if the *Show pictures* option is not selected.

- You have to remember that you have made these selections. If, for example, you find that picture content is not animated or that a video download has no effect, this will be because you have not selected these items in the Options – Advanced tab.

A lot of time can be wasted searching for items, and you should not have to search around for something that you have seen before. Internet Explorer has a History icon that can be clicked to present a list of items that you have contacted before, arranged in date order, with older items filed in the week in which they were used. You can set a limit to the time for which items are retained, and when you start using the Web you might want to make this 30 days or more. If you have once found an interesting item, you can return to it by using the History button and looking in the correct day or week list.

Another important time saver is the use of favourites. Internet Explorer maintains a Favorites folder, and shares it with Word-97 and other parts of the Microsoft Office set. You can make a sub-folder named NET and keep all your useful net addresses there. When you use the Favorites – Add to Favorites menu option you can specify which sub-folder you want to use, so that Net links are not mixed with Word or Excel documents.

Another way of treating links that you want to use many times is to place the net address in the Links bar by dragging it to this bar. You can make space by dragging unwanted items off the bar, and if you have too many links to display in one view, the bar can be scrolled by clicking on the arrowheads at either end.

The most important time (and telephone bill) savings can be made by using the File – Work Offline option of Internet Explorer. When this option is set, you can start Explorer without connecting to the Net, and you can review information that you have down-loaded earlier. When you need to connect, a pane will appear to give you the choice of remaining offline or connecting, and when you are online you can open links until you find what you want. You can then go offline again to read the downloaded information, so that you are not reading or printing while the telephone bill is ticking up costs.

While a page is being displayed, clicking on it with the right-hand mouse button provides a menu from which you can use Select All. With all the text of a page selected, you can right click again for the options of Print or Copy. Note that this applies to text only; you need to use the picture items on the menu if you want to save, copy or print a picture.

Glossary of terms

This is a small glossary that applies particularly to terms used in Windows and MS-DOS 6.0. For a full explanation of terms used in computing, see *Collins Dictionary of Personal Computing* by Ian Sinclair.

Active icon The Windows icon which has been clicked on and whose menu will appear on the next click.

Active printer The printer which will print out from your Windows work. Only one printer is active at a time, though several printers can be installed.

Active window The window in which you can make entries and select items. Other windows can display on the screen but do not respond to the use of keys until you switch to one of them. Programs can, however, continue to run inside an inactive window, carrying out actions such as searching and sorting which do not require your attention.

Application A program or suite of programs for a particular purpose such as a spreadsheet, wordprocessor, desktop publisher, CAD program, etc. The same word is sometimes used to mean programs that run under MS-DOS.

Application icon A Windows icon representing a program that appears outside a menu box on the main screen display, normally at the foot of the screen though it can be moved elsewhere. Clicking on these items will select a program to run, double clicking will start the program running.

Associate To nominate a file name extension as one created by an application, so that TXT might be associated with a wordprocessor, SKD with a CAD program, PUB with a DTP program and so on.

Attribute One of a set of markers in a file which can make the file read-only (the R attribute), archive (changed but not copied), system (essential to operation of computer) or hidden (not appearing in a folder listing).

AUTOEXEC.BAT file A file of text commands that is placed on the disk drive that the computer boots from, and which sets up various items before MS-DOS programs are run.

Background 1. The screen that is visible outside the current active window. 2. An inactive window or an icon whose program can be working without attention from the keyboard or mouse. A program working in the background can be sorting or searching data or exchanging text or other files with another computer.

Backup Any system for storing data over a long period, not part of the computer system. This includes floppy disks, data tapes, detachable hard drives and writeable CDs.

Binary file A file of coded numbers that are meaningless when printed or displayed but which convey information. A program is always in binary file form, but program control files such as CONFIG.SYS, AUTOEXEC.BAT and WIN.INI are in ordinary readable text form.

Bitmap A graphics image which is stored in the form of numbers that represent the intensity and colour of each part of the screen. A simple bitmap requires a lot of disk space, typically 100 Kbyte or more, for a screen. Other forms of file for graphics such as PCX compress this information considerably (if there are 500 consecutive red dots, for example, you need store only the information for one red dot along with the number of them).

Boot To start up the computer either from a system disk or from a hard disk. The act of booting always checks and clears the memory.

Branch A folder which is connected to the main (root) folder or which is a sub-folder or another folder.

Built-in font A font which is permanently contained in a printer and which can be used by any software, but mainly by MS-DOS. The view of text on the screen will not necessarily correspond to the appearance when printed unless the screen can use an identical font.

Cache A portion of memory used for temporary storage. A set of instruction codes to the processor can be read from normal memory or from disk into fast cache memory and fed to the processor at a much higher rate than could otherwise be achieved.

Cartridge A plug-in unit, such as the ink cartridge of an inkjet printer or the toner cartridge of a laser printer.

Cascade A set of windows which overlap but allow each title to be displayed so that it is possible to click on the top line of any one. Also applied to menus when one menu allows another to be opened with the first still visible.

Celerix A new trademark being used for the lower cost Pentium-II chips. There is a possibility that the Pentium name may be dropped because of the confusion caused by the number of different Pentium types. At the moment, it is uncertain of the Slot-1 fitting for Pentium-II will make the older Socket-7 obsolete, and much depends on whether other chip suppliers move to using Slot-1.

Check box A small square box that can contain an X or be blank, used in Windows to switch an option on or off.

Clicking The action of quickly pressing and releasing the button (usually the left-hand button) on the mouse.

Clicking on name/icon The action of placing a Windows cursor on a name or icon and then clicking the mouse button.

Clipboard The temporary storage for text or graphics used by Windows to copy data from one application to another, or from one part of an application to another.

Close To end the use of a window, either by double clicking on the control menu box, or by clicking on the control menu box and selecting Close from the menu.

COM 1. Abbreviation for Communication used to indicate a serial port. The COM ports are numbered as COM1, COM2, etc. 2. An extension for a short type of program file.

Command button The OK or Cancel word enclosed in a rectangular box and used to confirm or cancel a selection.

Communications settings The settings of speed and other factors that are needed to make serial transfer of files possible.

CONFIG.SYS file A file of text commands that imposes various settings on the computer before any programs, even MS-DOS itself, can be loaded. Changes to the CONFIG.SYS file have no effect until the machine is rebooted. You do not need to make use of CONFIG.SYS when you work solely with Windows.

Confirmation message A warning message that appears when you have chosen an action that might destroy files. You will be asked to confirm that you really intend to go ahead. Some confirmation messages can be turned off or restricted.

Control menu The menu that is available for each Windows application, allowing you to move the window, minimize, close, expand, etc.

Control menu icon The small icon at the left of the Windows title bar which is used to bring up the control menu (single click) or close the program (double click).

Copy To place a copy of some selected portion of a screen on to the Clipboard for pasting into another program or file. This leaves the original unchanged, unlike the Cut action.

Ctrl-Alt-Del The key combination that can be used to escape from a Windows program that appears to have locked up. Repeating the action will reboot the computer.

Cut To select a piece of text or graphics and transfer it to the Clipboard, removing it from the current window. Compare Copy.

Default A choice that is made for you, usually of the most likely option that will be needed. You need only confirm a default.

Desktop The full screen on which all the windows, icons and menu boxes will appear as you make use of Windows.

Desktop pattern A form of wallpaper which appears on the Windows desktop background so that you can distinguish the background more easily.

Dialog box A box which contains messages, or which require you to type an answer to a question that appears in the box.

Digitizer Any device that converts information into number code form. A digital camera and a scanner are both devices that will digitize an image, and a graphics tables can digitize a drawing. In this sense a keyboard is also a digitizer for alphabetical and numerical characters.

Disc A compact disc, also known as CD-ROM, whose data tracks can be used for text, sound or graphics. Multimedia programs are distributed in this form, which is also used for collections of graphics images and for other large programs.

Disk A magnetic disk, usually of the floppy type – the disks of a hard drive are called platters.

Double clicking The action used to select a program by placing the pointer over the program name and clicking the mouse button twice in rapid succession. This action is used much less in Windows 98 than in earlier versions.

Dragging The action of moving an object on screen by selecting it with the pointer, then holding the mouse button down and moving the mouse so as to move the object over the screen. The object is released when the mouse button is released. Some important dragging actions make use of auxiliary keys such as Shift, Ctrl or Alt.

Drag and drop The action of dragging a file icon to another icon such as the printer icon or a disk drive or folder icon and releasing the mouse button. When a file is dragged and dropped to the printer icon it will be printed (if it is printable and if the printer is on-line); when the file is dragged to a disk drive icon it will be copied to that drive.

Embedding The action of placing a drawing or an icon into a document, with the icon representing a another document or drawing. A document dealing with the topic of using the mouse, for example, might have a drawing between two paragraphs on the screen. Clicking on that drawing would allow you to edit it using the program that created the drawing. See also *Linking*.

Emulation The imitation of another device, such as a dot matrix printer emulating the control codes of another type, usually the Epson LQ or IBM ProPrinter types.

Expansion slot The socket (usually one of 4 to 8) within the computer which will accommodate a plug-in card that enhances the capabilities of the machine. Such slots are used for video cards, disk controller, network card and other add-on devices. The ISA slots run at a slow speed and can be used for comparatively slow devices such as ports and sound cards. Faster cards must use the PCI slots.

Extension The set of up to three letters following a full stop (period) in a file name. For example, in the name MYFILE.TXT, TXT is the extension. The extension letters of a file name are used to indicate the type of file. Windows 95/98 allows longer file names to be used, but the facility for an extension is retained.

Flow control A method of ensuring that serial data sent from one computer to another is synchronized, often by sending handshaking signals to indicate ready to send and ready to receive.

Font or fount A design of alphabetic or numerical characters, available in different sizes and styles (roman, bold, italic). Note that a font called Euro Collection can be obtained if you need to use the Euro symbol € in text.

Footer A piece of text that appears at the bottom of each printed page in a document.

Foreground 1. The part of the screen which contains the current active window. 2. The program which is currently under keyboard control and taking most of the processor time (see also Background).

Graphics resolution The measure of detail in a picture, in terms of dots per inch or dots per screen width. The higher the resolution the better the appearance, the longer it takes to print and the more memory it needs.

Handshake See Flow control.

Header A piece of text that appears at the top of each printed page in a document.

Highlight A method of marking an icon or text, using a different shading or colour.

Icon A graphics image that represents a program or menu selection which can be used (made active) by clicking the mouse button over the icon.

Inactive window A window which contains visible text or graphics but which is not currently being used by the mouse or keyboard.

Linking A form of embedding in which the embedded document or picture retains links to the program that created it. If you click on an icon for a linked picture, for example, you can edit the picture, and the new edited version will affect any other document linked to that icon – changing one copy changes all (in fact, there is only one copy, used by all the documents in which it is linked).

Local bus A set of connections between the processor chip and other components or cards that runs at a high clock rate and can be used for fast data transfer. The older ISA bus can be used for slower data interchange. The type of local bus used for Pentium machines is the PCI bus, but faster buses are being designed.

LPT An abbreviation of line printer, used to mean the parallel port (also indicated by PRN). When more than one parallel port is available, these will be numbered as LPT1, LPT2, etc.

Macro A recorded file of a set of actions, allowing the actions to be repeated by replaying the file. Many programs, such as Word for Windows or Lotus 1-2-3, contain their own macro system.

Mark To select text or programs.

Maximize The action of making a window expand to fill the screen. This can be done from the Control menu, or by clicking on the up arrow at the right of the title bar.

Memory resident (or TSR) A program which is loaded and remains in the memory of the computer rather than being run and discarded as most programs are. Such a program can be called into use by a key combination (a hot key like Print Screen), or it can permanently affect the machine until it is switched off (like KEYB).

MIDI An acronym of Musical Instrument Digital Interface, a system for allowing a computer to control electronic musical instruments. Windows provides for such control by way of sound files, but only if a suitable sound card is added in an expansion slot of the computer, and the appropriate instruments connected.

Minimize The action of shrinking a window and the program in it to an icon.

Modem A device which converts computer signals into musical tones and vice versa, allowing such signals to be transmitted along telephone lines.

Motherboard The main board of a computer, into which expansion cards, replacement processor, and memory chips can be plugged. Many machines allow the whole motherboard to be swapped so that the machine can be upgraded.

Mouse The small trolley whose movement on the desk controls the movement of a pointer or other indicator on the screen. The use of the mouse is central to Windows.

OLE Object linking and embedding, see Linking, Embedding, Packaging.

Packaging The use of an icon to represent a piece of text or a drawing so that it can be embedded or linked in another document. When the document is printed, the icon is printed, but double clicking on the icon when the document is on screen will show the packaged material. Packaging allows a program that cannot be used directly for embedding or linking to have its files represented as icons in this way.

Parallel port The connector used for printers which sends data signals along a set of cables, eight data signals at a time. Also called a Centronics port.

Parameter A piece of information needed to complete a command. For example, a COPY command would need as parameters the name of the file to be copied and the destination to which it had to be copied.

Parity A crude system of checking memory by using an additional bit as a check. At a time when memory was unreliable, parity was used on all PC machines, so that each byte of data used nine bits rather than eight. This precaution is no longer needed, and modern computers dispense with parity, making memory cheaper.

Paste To copy a piece of text or graphics from the Clipboard into a window.

Pixel A unit of screen display, a dot, whose brightness and/or colour can be controlled. Nothing smaller than one pixel can be displayed.

Platter An aluminium disk coated with magnetic material and used within a hard drive for storing digital information.

PnP Abbreviation of plug and play, a system of hardware card design that allows a card to be plugged into a modern computer and used without the need to set jumpers.

Point size A printers unit of type size, equal to 1/72 inch.

Pointer The shape on the screen that moves as you move the mouse. Windows uses several different shapes of pointers to indicate that the pointer will have a different action when it is over a different part of a window. Some programs that run under the control of Windows will use other pointer shapes in addition to these types.

Printer driver A program that determines how the printer makes use of the codes that are sent from the computer – using the wrong printer driver will result in very strange printed output, because different printers use different methods. Many dot matrix printers, however, use Epson codes, and many laser printers use either Hewlett-Packard Laserjet codes or the universal PostScript system (from Adobe Corp.).

Proportional font A font in which the spacing between letters is varied according to the space needed by each letter.

Reboot Restarting the computer either by using the Ctrl-Alt-Del keys (a soft reboot) or by pressing the RESET key (a hard reboot). Either will wipe all programs and data from the memory.

Restore button The button that is placed at the right-hand side of the title bar when a window has been maximized – clicking on this button will restore the former size.

Screen font A font that appears on the screen to indicate or simulate the font that has been selected for the printer.

Scroll bars The bars at the right-hand side and bottom of a window. Dragging the button in the scroll bar performs the action of moving the window over the text or picture, allowing a different portion to be viewed.

Select To choose an action by clicking its icon (another click needed to run it) or to mark text or graphics for cutting.

Serial port The connector used for sending or receiving data one bit at a time. This is used mainly for connecting computers to each other, either directly or by way of a modem through telephone lines. A few printers require a serial port connection, many others allow it as an option. The serial ports are referred to by the letters COM.

Soft font A font which is not built in or in cartridge form, but sent as a file from the computer to a printer, and needs to be loaded again after either the printer or the computer has been switched off. Such a font can be made to appear in identical forms both on screen and on paper.

Sound card An add-on card that fits into an expansion slot allowing sound outputs to be taken to amplifiers and loudspeakers (some cards incorporate a small amount of amplification). Such a card, of which SoundBlaster is typical, allows sound effects to be incorporated into Windows actions.

Spool To store printer information in memory so that it can be fed out to the printer while the computer gets on with other actions. If a lot of text needs to be spooled, it is useful to allow the spooling to take place in expanded or extended memory.

Swap file Part of the hard disk used in Windows to swap with memory so that the memory is not overloaded.

Text file A file that contains only a limited selection of codes for the letters of the alphabet, digits and punctuation marks.

Tiling An arrangement of windows in which there is no overlapping, unlike Cascade.

Title bar The strip at the top of a window that contains the title of the application, and also the control box and minimize/maximize arrows.

TrueType font A form of soft font packaged with Windows 3.1 which presents the same appearance on the screen as on paper, allowing you to be much more certain that what you see is what you eventually get. The extension letters TTF are used for font files.

Vector font A font that consists of instructions to draw lines, as distinct from a bit-map, which is a pattern of dots. A vector font can be easily scaled to any size.

Virtual machine Referring to the use of memory organized by Windows so that each application can be run in its own portion of memory

Virtual memory The use of a hard disk by Windows as if it were part of the memory of the computer.

Windows application A program that has been designed to run within Windows, and which will not run unless Windows is being used. All such programs present the same pattern of controls (the user interface) making them easier to learn.

Abbreviations and acronyms

AGP Accelerated Graphics Port, a very fast slot for graphics cards of the AGP type.

ANSI American National Standards Institute, the title is used for a number code system that follows the ASCII set for numbers 32 to 127, and specifies characters for the set 128 to 255.

ASCII American Standard Code for Information Interchange, the number code for letters, numerals and punctuation marks that uses the numbers 32 to 127. Text files are normally ASCII or ANSI coded.

AT Advanced Technology, the designation used by IBM in 1982 for the computer that succeeded the older PC-XT.

ATA AT Attachment, a device intended to connect to the AT bus such as an IDE hard drive.

ATX AT Extended, a new design of casing, power supply and motherboard that simplifies connections and component positioning, improves cooling and provides low voltage supplies.

BIOS Basic Input Output System, the program in a ROM chip that allows the computer to make use of screen, disk and keyboard, and which can read in the operating system.

CAD Computer Aided Design, a program that allows the computer to produce technical drawings to scale.

CD-ROM A form of read-only memory, consisting of a compact disc whose digital information can be read as a set of files.

CGA Colour Graphics Adapter, the first IBM attempt to produce a video graphics card.

CISC Complex Instruction Set Chip, a microprocessor which can act on any of a very large number (typically more than 300) instructions. All of the Intel microprocessors to date are of this type. See also RISC.

CMOS Complementary Metal-Oxide Semiconductor, a form of chip construction that requires a very low current. As applied to memory, a chip that allows its contents to be retained by applying a low voltage at negligible current.

CP/M Control, Program, Monitor, one of the first standard operating systems for small computers.

CPU Central Processing Unit, the main microprocessor chip of a computer.

CRT Cathode Ray Tube, the display device for monitors used with desktop machines.

CTS Clear To Send, the companion handshake signal to RTS in the RS-232 system.

DCE Data Communications Equipment, a device such as a computer that send out serial data along a line.

DIL Dual In Line, a pin arrangement for chips that uses two sets of parallel pins.

DIP Dual in Line Package, a set of miniature switches arranged in the same form of package as a DIL chip.

DOS Disk Operating System, the programs that provides the commands that make a computer usable.

DSR Data Set Ready, another form of handshaking signal for RS-232.

DTE Data Terminal Equipment, a receiver of serial data such as a modem.

DTR Data Terminal Ready, the RS232 companion signals to DSR.

DTP Desktop Publishing, the use of a computer for composing type and graphics into book or newspaper pages.

EGA Enhanced Graphics Adapter, the improved form of graphics card introduced by IBM to replace CGA.

EISA Enhanced Industry Standard Architecture, a system for connecting chips in a PC machine which allows faster signal interchange than the standard (ISA) method that has been used since the early PC/AT models.

EMS Expanded Memory System, the original standard for adding memory to the PC/XT machine, now seldom used.

ISDN Integrated Signals Digital Network, a system of cabling, often using fibre optics, that is used for high-speed digital links for computing and for digital sound and video links.

LCD Liquid Crystal Display, a form of shadow display which is used on calculators and portable computers. It depends on the action of materials to polarize light when an electrical voltage is applied.

LCS Liquid Crystal Shutter, an array of LCD elements used to control light and so expose the light-sensitive drum in a laser printer. The LCD bar is used as an alternative to the use of a laser beam.

LED Light Emitting Diode, a device used for warning lights, and also as a form of light source in laser-style printers.

MCA Micro Channel Architecture, a system proposed and used at one time by IBM as a way of connecting chips within a computer, intended to replace the AT-bus (ISA).

MDA Monochrome Display Adapter, the first type of video card used in IBM PC machines.

MIDI Musical Instrument Digital Interface, a standard form of serial data code used to allow electronic instruments to be controlled by a computer, or to link them with each other.

MS-DOS   Microsoft Disk Operating System, the standard operating system for the PC type of machine.

NTSC   National Television Standards Committee, the body that drew up the specification for the colour TV system used in the USA and Japan since 1952.

OCR   Optical Character Recognition, software that can be used on a scanned image file to convert images of characters into ASCII codes.

OS/2   An operating system devised by IBM and intended to replace PC-DOS (the IBM version of MS-DOS).

PAL   Phase Alternating Line, the colour TV system devised by Telefunken in Germany and used throughout Europe apart from France.

PCI   PC Interconnection, a fast form of local bus used for speed-critical cards such as graphics and video cards.

PBX   Private Branch Exchange, sometimes a problem for using modems.

PSS   Packet Switch Stream, a method of transmitting digital signals efficiently along telephone lines.

RAM   Random Access Memory. All memory is random access, but this acronym is used to mean read-write as distinct from read-only memory.

RGB   Red Green Blue, the three primary colour TV signals. A monitor described as RGB needs to be supplied with three separate colour signals, unlike a monitor that can use a composite signal.

RISC   A microprocessor that can work with only a few simple instructions, each of which can be completed very rapidly.

RLL   Run Length Limited, a form of high-density recording for hard disks.

ROM   Read-Only Memory, the form of non-volatile memory that is not erased when the power is switched off.

RS232 The old standard for serial communications.

RTS Request to Send, a handshaking signal for RS-232.

SCART The standard form of connector for video equipment, used on TV receivers and video recorders.

SCSI Small Computer Systems Interface, a form of fast-acting disk drive interface which allows for almost unlimited expansion. Used mainly on Mac machines, but also found (in a less standardized form) for some PC devices.

SECAM Séquence Couleur et Mémoire, the French colour TV system, also used in Eastern Europe and the countries of the former USSR.

SIMM Single Inline Memory Module, a slim card carrying memory chips, used for inserting memory in units of 1 Mbyte or 4 Mbyte.

SMART Self Monitoring and Reporting Technology, used on hard drives so that they can check and report on faults or potential faults.

TIFF Tagged Image File Format, one method of coding graphics images that is widely used by scanners.

TSR Terminate and Stay Resident, a form of program that runs and remains in the memory to influence the computer.

TTL Transistor-Transistor Logic, a family of digital chips. The name is often used to mean that a device will work on 0 and +5 V levels.

UPS Uninterruptible Power Supply, a unit using batteries that will provide power to the PC for a limited time when mains power fails. The UPS will keep the computer running long enough to shut down all files and switch off, and the UPS batteries will be recharged when mains power is restored.

VDU Visual Display Unit, another name for the monitor.

VEGA Video Extended Graphics Association, a group of US manufacturers who have agreed on a common standard for high-resolution graphics cards.

VGA Video Graphics Array, the video card introduced by IBM for their PS/2 range of computers.

Hexadecimal number scale

All computing depends on the use of number codes. Some of the numbers are used to refer to locations in memory, each of which is numbered; some are used to mean commands, characters (using ASCII code) and other references. Each of these numbers is internally a set of 1s and 0s. Binary code like this is fine for machines, because with only two possibilities to work with, the chances of the machine making a mistake become very remote. Humans, however, are not ideally suited to working in binary numbers without making mistakes, simply because the stream of 1s and 0s becomes confusing, and an obvious step is to use a more convenient number scale.

Just what is a more convenient number scale is quite another matter. Most people work with the ordinary 0 to 9 scale of denary numbers, based on counting in tens. Memory analysing programs like Microsoft's MSD, and memory management programs of all types, however, are written more for the convenience of professional programmers, who use hexadecimal numbers, as for the ordinary computer user. Hexadecimal means scale of sixteen, and the reason that it is used so extensively is that it is naturally suited to representing binary bytes.

Four bits, half of a byte, will represent numbers which lie in the range 0 to 15 in our ordinary number scale. This is the range of

Denary	Hex	Denary	Hex
0	00	8	08
1	01	9	09
2	02	10	0A
3	03	11	0B
4	04	12	0C
5	05	13	0D
6	06	14	0E
7	07	15	0F

A.1 The hexadecimal number scale.

one hex digit (Figure A.1). Since we don't have symbols for digits higher than 9, we have to use the letters A, B, C, D, E, and F to supplement the digits 0 to 9 in the hex scale. The advantage is that a byte of data can be represented by a two digit number, and a complete address by a five digit number.

Converting between binary and hex is much simpler than converting between binary and denary. The number that we write as 10 (ten) in denary is written as 0A in hex, eleven as 0B, twelve as 0C and so on up to fifteen, which is 0F. The zero doesn't have to be written, but programmers get into the habit of writing a data byte with two digits and an address with four or more even if fewer digits are needed. The number that follows 0F is 10, sixteen in denary, and the scale then repeats to 1F, thirty-one, which is followed by 20. The maximum size of byte, 255 in denary, is FF in hex.

When we write hex numbers, it's usual to mark them in some way so that you don't confuse them with denary numbers. There's not much chance of confusing a number like 3E with a denary number, but a number like 26 might be hex or denary. The convention that is followed by many programmers is to use a capital H to mark a hex number, with the H sign placed after the number. Most of the MS-DOS memory utilities assume that you will type in hex numbers, and they will not work with anything else, and addresses in MSD make use of hex numbers also.

Before we can get much further with addresses and their contents, we need to look at the way that addresses are organized. Because the 8088 and 8086 chips were developed from the older 8-bit 8088 type, there has been a strong family resemblance, and one thing that has carried over is the storing of numbers in 16-bit units, one word units, used also in later chips. Now one word of 16 bits can represent a scale of ten numbers from 0 to 65 536, which is hex 0000H to FFFFH, a range of 64 Kbyte, but the construction of the 8088, 8086 and 80286 chips allowed for the use of 20-bit numbers for addresses. This makes the hex range of numbers 00000 to FFFFF, 0 to 1 048 575. By contrast, the Pentium processors use 32-bit numbers, so that the address range is 00000000 to FFFFFFFF, and future processors are likely to use 64-bit numbering which translates to 16-digit hex numbers.

Index

Loudspeaker, 18
Luminance, 65

Magazines, 6
Magneto-optical, 120
Mail order, 6
Manual, modem, 164
Manuals, motherboard, 30
Marking sectors, 43
Master, 51
Maximize, 148
Maximum memory, 33
MDS display, 70
Media player software, 124
Memory installation, 32
Memory, laser printer, 156
Menu bar, 148
Metal case, 15
Microprocessor, 2
Minimize, 148
MMX chip, 8
MO technology, 120
Modem, 160
Modem connection, 84
Modulation, 165
Monitor, 59
Monitor, professional, 61
Mono monitor, 61
Motherboard, 8, 19
Motherboard assembly, 33
Motherboard preparation, 29
Mounting bolts, 36
Mounting brackets, drive, 49
Mounting holes, motherboard, 34
Mounting pads, drive, 50
Mouse ports, 76
Mouse, 85
MSCDEX.EXE driver, 43, 122
MS-DOS tracks, 42
MS-DOS, 2
Multimedia, 116, 121
Multisync monitor, 69

Needs, 2
Networks, 131
Non-interlaced monitor, 69
Non-modem cable, 134
NTSC system, 67
Null-modem connection, 84

OCR, 127
Older components, 5
On/off switch, 18
Opening window, 147
Other manufacturers, chips, 9
Overclocking, 31

Package, sound-board, 124
PAL system, 67
Paper, laser printer, 157
Parallel port, 78
Parallel printer, 153
Parity, 162
Partition, 100
Password options, 96
Payment, protected, 6
PC machine, 1
PC/AT machine, 2
PCI slots, 23
PCI sound card, 126
Pentium, 8
Phase shift, 166
Phosphors, 62
Photo-real printing, 159
Piezo inkjet, 155
Pillars, support, 19
Pin 1
indication, 54
Pixels, 61
Plastic casing, 15
Platters, 44
Plug and Play, 81
Plugs for drives, 25
Port upgrade, 111
Portable computers, 7
Ports, 76